TOUCHED BY POWERS MYSTERIOUS AND GLORIOUS

He won the Nobel Prize for his scientific achievements but never forgot the miracle that made him believe in a power beyond science . . .

A psychic told her she would find the love she sought, but it took a biblical message to show her the way . . .

A Native American who had been prepared for burial arose and announced he had died and gone to the gates of Heaven. There an angel had sent him back with a message important to all Native Americans . . .

And a couple who were told that it was impossible for them to ever have a child gave birth to Paul Robert Walker, who grew up to document his and other extraordinary stories in

EVERY DAY'S A MIRACLE

EVERY DAY'S
A MIRACLE

PAUL ROBERT WALKER

AVON BOOKS  NEW YORK

EVERY DAY'S A MIRACLE is an original publication of Avon Books. This work has never before appeared in book form.

AVON BOOKS
A division of
The Hearst Corporation
1350 Avenue of the Americas
New York, New York 10019

Copyright © 1995 by Paul Robert Walker
Published by arrangement with the author
Library of Congress Catalog Card Number: 95-94484
ISBN: 0-380-78069-0

First Avon Books Printing: December 1995

AVON TRADEMARK REG. U.S. PAT. OFF. AND IN OTHER COUNTRIES, MARCA REGISTRADA, HECHO EN U.S.A.

Printed in the U.S.A.

RA 10 9 8 7 6 5 4 3

To Marlene, Devin, and Dariel
—my greatest miracles

CONTENTS

Contents

FOREWORD

Bob and Elsie were an ideal couple—intelligent, attractive, and very much in love. Bob was a war hero, a dive-bomber pilot who had been shot down over the South Pacific and lived to tell the tale. When the war ended, Elsie had rejected a job offer as a newspaper reporter so that she and Bob could settle down and start their family. Now it was 1952. They owned a successful dry goods store on the west side of Chicago and went home each evening to a cute little house in the nearby suburb of River Grove. Everything was perfect—except they couldn't have children.

They had been married for ten years now and had never used birth control. Of course, there had been the years of separation during the war, but the war had been over for a long time, and the closest they'd ever come to having a child was a miscarriage in the first trimester. The doctor said there was something wrong with Elsie's womb—it just wouldn't hold the egg. He wasn't very clear about it, but he wasn't encouraging, either. He suggested that they consider adoption.

Bob and Elsie weren't getting any younger, and they agreed that it was unrealistic to keep hoping for a miracle. So they decided to adopt a child. But where would they apply? Most adoption agencies were run by religious organizations, and they required that both parents share the same faith. Bob was raised a Catholic. He didn't have much use for all the rules and regulations, but he loved the mystical spirituality of the Church, and he hoped that their child would be raised a Catholic. Elsie had been baptized a Lutheran, but her family was never very religious at all. Though Bob wouldn't say it out loud, the feeling was that perhaps Elsie should convert.

One summer evening Elsie decided to attend a lecture at a Catholic church in a neighboring suburb. "I was just curious," she says today. "Some people go to a lecture on China. I decided to go to a lecture on Catholicism." With her keen reporter's instincts, Elsie asked lots of tough, probing questions—mostly about the strict rules and "hocus-pocus" of the Church. The bright young priest who gave the lecture impressed her with his intelligent, insightful responses. She left the lecture intrigued, but not convinced.

Elsie had always felt that something was missing from her spiritual life, but even more compelling was the child who was missing from their family life. If she became a Catholic, they could adopt through Catholic Charities. For several days, she played these issues over in her mind, until one day—almost as if she were operating on automatic pilot—she looked up the local Catholic church in the phone book and made arrangements to take conversion lessons.

Right from the start, Elsie liked Father Ryan, her teacher and the pastor of St. Cyprian Parish. He was a big, smiling, red-faced Irishman with a shock of gray hair and a belly that spoke of good food and drink. His blue eyes shined with a piercing intelligence, and his heart held a deep, abiding goodness. He had already heard about Elsie; the young priest who gave the lecture had called to tell him that he had "a real live one in River Grove." Father Ryan laughed good-naturedly at Elsie's skeptical questions and did his best to explain what really mattered. And what really mattered, he said, was very simple and very beautiful: love, faith, and hope. The rest was window dressing.

At their very first meeting, Father Ryan helped Elsie make out the adoption application for Catholic Charities. But even as they filled out the papers, she admitted that she desperately longed for a natural child of her own. It was more than longing, really—it was a painful, palpable desire to carry a child in her womb, no matter what the doctor said. Father Ryan spoke to her of Mary, the mother of Jesus. Surely, the Blessed Mother understood the longing that Elsie felt within her womb.

In early November 1952, after several months of instruction, Elsie made a novena to Mary. A novena is a series of nine Masses, considered the most powerful form of prayer in all the rituals of the Catholic Church. On the first night of the novena, Father Ryan greeted Elsie outside the church and looked directly into her eyes. "Hello, Elsie," he said with a warm smile. "Now don't forget to pray for whatever you want." Of course Father Ryan knew what Elsie wanted.

That night during the Mass, Elsie offered her silent prayer. "O Mother Mary, you have felt the pangs of childhood and fullness of the womb. I too want a child, but my womb is empty. The doctor says I am barren. But I know it is within your power to intercede for me with your Son who can do all things. If it is God's plan that I should carry a child in my own womb, then I pray that it be soon, while I am young enough to give that child all the care and love he will need. If my empty womb is the will of God, then so be it. I accept His judgment, and I will adopt a stranger's child and give that child all the love I have."

For a long moment, Elsie knelt with her eyes closed in absolute stillness. When she opened them again, she felt as if a great weight had been lifted from her spirit. It was out of her hands now. She had passed the burden to Mary, the Blessed Mother of Jesus. What would be, would be.

Exactly nine months later, on August 5, 1953, Elsie gave birth to a healthy baby boy. The joy she felt when she held the baby in her arms—her own baby, the fruit of her own womb—transcended any joy she had ever hoped for, or imagined. Now she felt complete. Now Elsie, Bob, and the baby were a family.

Father Ryan came to visit as soon as the mother and child were out of the hospital. It was less than a year since he and Elsie had begun their lessons, but in that short time the old priest had been stricken with cancer. He no longer had the strength to carry the daily load of his pastoral duties, but he told Bob and Elsie that he would baptize this child. For this child was living proof of the power of prayer.

One life begins and another life ends. That winter, Father Ryan died. He lived just long enough to see another prayer answered—the completion of a new church for his parish, the great labor of his final years. For most parishioners, it seemed a fitting monument to a good-hearted man of faith. But for Elsie, the beautiful new church seemed empty without the red-faced Irish priest who had understood her deepest desire and guided her to express that desire in prayer.

On Easter Sunday, the first Easter since Father Ryan had died, Elsie attended Mass in the new church. Halfway through the service, she bowed her head and recited the ritual Latin prayers. When she raised her eyes to look at the altar, the face of Father Ryan filled the entire sanctuary! His priestly cassock rose from the communion rail and his kind smile stretched across the altar; his wise, twinkling eyes floated like heavenly orbs above the candles; his shock of gray hair brushed the ceiling.

Elsie looked around to see if anyone else saw it, but the rest of the congregation went on with the Mass, unaware of this miracle in their midst. It was a special vision just for her, a message from eternity. Elsie's initial surprise turned to warm, overflowing peace, as she felt herself wrapped in the smile of her teacher, her friend. Everything is so simple, she thought, if we leave our problems in the hands of God.

And so it is—then, now, and forever. The boy who was born on the wings of Elsie's prayer, the boy who was baptized by Father Ryan, was named Paul Robert Walker. I am that boy. And I believe in miracles.

I don't remember when my mother first told me this story, but it seems as if it has always been there, infusing my life with a sweet, mystical resonance. Am I a mystic? No, not really. But I believe that there is more to this life than meets the eye, more than can be explained by natural laws—or at least by the natural laws that we currently understand. Although I have endless faith in human potential, I believe in a power greater than our own, a power that most of us call God. And I believe that there are special moments when this power touches us profoundly and elevates us beyond the natural reality of the earthly world. I believe these moments are miracles.

This book includes fifty-two true stories of miraculous experiences, great and small, secular and sacred. The stories are arranged in twelve chapters representing the twelve months of the year—a reminder that miracles happen every day. Whenever a miracle occurred on a specific date or in a specific month, I have placed the story in the chapter devoted to that month. But when the exact month is unknown, or when the miraculous events occurred over many months, I've used my own subjective judgment in placing the story. The stories within each month are also arranged subjectively.

Most of these stories are contemporary, and many are published here for the first time, but I've also included some historical miracles that might have special interest for the modern reader. When the facts of a story have been previously published—whether historical or contemporary—I've tried to offer a new perspective by comparing various sources or obtaining new information through personal interviews. The newly-published miracles come from personal interviews and correspondence, including electronic mail from a wide range of people that I've met through on-line bulletin boards.

I am not an investigative reporter; I am a storyteller. I believe that the stories I tell in this book are true, because they were told to me by sane, solid people of good faith and good heart—people who have no reason to fabricate a miracle in order to please me or anyone else. In fact, many sources have had to overcome a natural reticence in order to openly admit that they've been touched by the miraculous. With deep respect for the courage of my sources and the intelligence of my readers, I have tried to tell each story as truthfully as I could, and wherever possible I've checked and rechecked the facts with the key people involved.

Nobel laureate Dr. Alexis Carrel—whose own story is told in this book—once wrote that it was "distressingly unpleasant to be personally involved in a miracle." Carrel's distress grew out of his education in the western scientific method, for by its very nature, a miracle is an event that cannot be readily explained by science. My own view, however, is that science and miracles can, and do, exist side-by-side. The only conflict arises when we place too much faith in science, when we believe that science is the final answer, the absolute power of the universe. It isn't, and it never will be—which brings us back to God.

The stories in this book represent a variety of religious beliefs, and some stories unfold with no religious context at all. Yet religious issues dance in and around them as surely as thoughts dance in the human mind. For my part, I have tried to avoid theological interpretations and to present the stories as stories—miraculous events in the lives of human beings. But I know that most readers will see these events through the filter of their own beliefs, and despite my efforts at objectivity, I cannot help but tell the stories through the filter of my own beliefs.

I follow no formal religion, though I respect those who do. Yet, I consider myself a profoundly religious person. Years ago, I discovered a metaphor for the diversity of religious belief, a metaphor that still makes sense to me today. I wish I could give credit where credit is due, but I don't remember the source of this image. So I pass it on to you as I see it in my own mind:

I believe that God—the ultimate, transcendent power of the universe—is like the peak of a mountain, and the religions of the world are paths up the sides of that mountain, all leading toward God. At the beginning of the journey—the base of the mountain—these paths seem very far apart. And as we begin to climb, we each see different landscapes, different features, depending upon the path we have chosen. But as we continue to ascend, the paths converge, drawing closer together until they meet at the peak and become one in God. The upper regions of the mountain are the realm of the mystic, the realm of the miraculous.

Most of my sources are mentioned in the stories themselves or in the introductory passages that I have included where appropriate. But I would like to acknowledge a few sources that are not mentioned elsewhere in the book. My editor, Stephen S. Power, who had the original idea for this book in a somewhat different form, has shown extraordinary literary generosity in allowing me to explore and develop the project on my own terms. My mother, Elsie, and my sister, Laurie, have both been extremely supportive, not only in affirming their deep interest in the subject, but also in referring friends to me whose stories are told in the book. My wife's grandmother, Lillian Fisher, has also been very helpful in offering stories.

I would also like to mention several written sources that were particularly useful. *Miracles* by D. Scott Rogo provided an excellent overview of the subject and led me toward many other sources. *Encountering Mary* by Sandra L. Zimdars-Swartz is an authoritative volume on Marian apparitions, and *Lourdes: A Modern Pilgrimage* by Patrick Marnham is an excellent discussion of that particular phenomenon. Two books by the Jesuit theologian Herbert Thurston, *Surprising Mystics* and *The Physical Phenomena of Mysticism,* offer a careful, cautiously skeptical analysis of miracles attributed to Catholic mystics.

Finally, I would like to thank you, the reader, for opening your heart and mind to these extraordinary stories. I pray that you and yours will always be touched by miracles.

JANUARY

Can any man dictate to God when he is to speak?
Or command him to make proclamation?
At one moment the light is not seen,
it is overcast with clouds and rain;
Then the wind passes by and clears them away,
and a golden glow comes from the north.

—THE BOOK OF JOB

THE MEANING OF
SURVIVAL

In early January 1991, Sam Zelikson was walking back from lunch to his glass-and-mirror business in the Bronx. It was a gray winter's day, with a steady cold rain falling on the city. As Sam crossed the street in front of his shop, a motorist jumped the light and gunned her car into the intersection, smashing his body and throwing the sixty-two-year-old man twenty feet into the air. When he landed on the hard asphalt, he was bloody, limp, and unconscious.

From a police station around the corner, two policemen quickly arrived at the scene of the accident. Sam's partner, Uly, was there to hear the first policeman's grim assessment of the situation:

"Forget it. Call the morgue. He's gone."

But the second policeman didn't see it that way. "He's still breathing! Call the ambulance!"

The ambulance rushed Sam to a nearby hospital, where the emergency room team revived him, and he began the process of recovery. No one who really knew Sam Zelikson ever had a doubt that he *would* recover. It would take more that an auto accident to stop a man like him. For if a single word can describe a human being, the word that describes Sam Zelikson is survivor.

Fifty years earlier, as a twelve-year-old boy in his native Latvia, Sam had survived the horrors of the Dvinsk Ghetto, where the Nazis rounded up the Jews. One day a guard kicked Sam for being slow to light a fire. When Sam's father complained, the guard shot the older man on the spot, right before the eyes of his family. Later, Sam and his mother jumped from a freight car on the way to their own execution. Hiding in the dense Latvian forest, they watched the Nazis machine-gun thousands of Jews—including Sam's older brother—in front of an open pit.

After Sam and his mother were recaptured and returned to the ghetto, the guards decided who would live and who would die. As they measured the height of the prisoners, Sam stood on top of his shoes to make himself appear taller. The guard ordered Sam to the right, but his mother and two younger brothers were sent to the left, where they boarded one of six buses that they believed would take them to another camp. Instead, as Sam gazed through the windows of the bus, he heard the soft hissing of gas and watched the rest of his family die.

Alone in the world, Sam Zelikson escaped and hid in the local cemetery, digging up corpses and gnawing on their bones to survive—only to be recaptured and sent to five concentration camps . . . where he stayed alive by sharp wits and brutal work, including long shifts in the crematorium, burning the bodies of the dead.

Sam was liberated in early 1945 and came to America four years later. Life got better, but there were still hard times. He mangled his hand while installing a plate of glass and broke both his legs in a fall from a window. He broke a leg right before his wedding, too, and wore a huge cast on his Niagara Falls honeymoon. Despite their rough start, Sam and his wife, Janice, enjoyed a long, happy marriage with five beloved children—four daughters and a son. Sam's family was his greatest joy. Yet no matter how good life seemed, sorrow followed Sam like a dark shadow of the past. In 1986, his son Barry died of cancer at the age of twenty-six.

Sam never really got over Barry's death. But he did what he always did. He survived. He went on with his life and kept Barry alive in his heart.

After the auto accident, Sam spent three weeks in the

hospital, recovering slowly. He complained of pain in his ribs, but the doctor said that the X-rays showed no broken bones—amazing considering how high he had been thrown into the air by the onrushing car. He had problems with his neck as well. He could turn it to the right, but not to the left. Nonetheless, the doctor allowed him to go home to his family.

Sam was scheduled to be released from the hospital on Saturday, January 26. That morning, he lay in his bed, saying his prayers. Throughout all his misfortunes—from the Holocaust to the accident in the Bronx—Sam Zelikson had never lost his faith in God. He felt a special, direct connection to heaven whenever he prayed. Since Barry's death, Sam often focused on his son in his prayers, but on this particular morning, Sam felt Barry's presence more powerfully than usual. It was almost as if Barry was right there in the room beside him.

As Sam finished praying, his roommate spoke up from the other hospital bed. "Hey Sam," he said, "the lottery's up to ninety million!"

At that moment, Sam felt someone push his hand. The push was very strong and very solid, but there was no one there. At least no one he could see. Sam smiled. He felt sure that it was Barry, letting him know that everything was going to be all right—and telling him to play the lottery.

Sam had been playing the lottery regularly for years. He'd never won much of anything—his biggest windfall was a grand total of four hundred and eighty dollars—but he enjoyed it and he could afford a few bucks every week. Of course he hadn't thought much about the lottery while he was in the hospital. But now that he was getting out, it seemed like a perfect way to celebrate his homecoming. And the push from Barry made it seem even more perfect.

When his wife and daughters arrived to take him home, Sam said, "Today's a ninety-million lotto. Are we gonna play?"

"No," his daughter Linda replied. "First, we're gonna get you home."

They drove Sam back to their house in Yonkers—the house where they'd lived for twenty-seven years. It would have been easy to forget about the lottery and enjoy being back in the warm embrace of his family. But Sam insisted on playing. The family joined in, with everyone picking out their favorite numbers—the day Sam was liberated from the last concentration camp, Sam and Janice's wedding anniversary, their children's birthdays. Finally, when everyone had their numbers, Sam took sixteen dollars out of his pocket and handed it to Linda, who went out with her sister Alice to buy the tickets.

That evening, the family sat in front of the television, watching as the winning numbers were drawn. When the first four numbers matched four numbers on one of the tickets, Sam started getting a little excited. "At least, we're in the money," he said, thinking maybe they'd win a few hundred dollars or so. Then the fifth number matched the same ticket. Now they were looking at a few thousand dollars. But there was still one more number. Just one more.

The Zelikson family held their breath as the sixth number came up. It matched! Sam looked at the ticket again just to make sure. There it was plain as day. All six numbers.

"What am I gonna do with ninety million dollars?" he asked.

As it turned out, Sam never had to answer that question—at least not exactly. The Zeliksons shared the ninety-million-dollar jackpot with eight other winners, and each winning ticket paid a little more than ten million dollars. For twenty-one years, Sam and his family would receive an annual payment of $476,857 before taxes, $342,857 after taxes.

The first thing Sam did after winning the lottery was go back into the hospital—a different hospital closer to his home, where his own doctor was on the staff. A new set of X-rays showed that Sam had two broken ribs, just as he had suspected all along. After three more weeks in the hospital, he was released again, but this time he felt much better than he had the first time. As soon as he was strong enough, the whole Zelikson family went to Israel, where

Sam told his story for documentation in the archives of the Yad Vashem Holocaust Museum.

When they returned from the trip, the Zeliksons moved from their home in Yonkers to a new home in the upscale suburb of Chappaqua. After a lifetime of hard work, Sam retired from his glass-and-mirror business, leaving it in the capable hands of his partner, Uly. Today, the family uses part of their windfall to help others less fortunate than themselves. They also enjoy vacations together, and wherever they travel—Hawaii, the Caribbean, or Europe—Sam always feels that Barry is there watching over them, happy at their good fortune.

In May 1995, as this manuscript was nearing completion, Sam took care of some unfinished business. In Judaism, a boy's bar mitzvah marks his arrival at religious and legal maturity. Most Jewish boys are bar mitzvahed at the age of thirteen, but Sam never had the opportunity because he was imprisoned at that time in the camps. So at the age of sixty-five, during the fiftieth year after the end of World War II and the liberation of the concentration camps, Sam was finally bar mitzvahed.

Sam Zelikson believes that his lottery win was a miracle in which Barry tried to give him something to make up for the suffering of the past. But he also believes that the lottery is only a small part of the story. The real miracle is his life. As Sam himself says, "It's about the meaning of survival."

ANGELS IN THE MIST

IN JANUARY 1978, DALE AND CHANTAL WERE DRIVING along the rugged Oregon coast, on their way home to San Diego after visiting Dale's cousin in Eugene. Dale in his early thirties, she in her late twenties, they were engaged to be married and looking forward to a lifetime together.

As they passed a sign that read "Lookout Point," Dale pulled over to the side of the road. "There's a great hike to the top of this mountain," he said. "I've been up there, but no one's ever climbed with me. Do you want to try it?"

"Sure," Chantal replied. "Sounds like fun." Chantal wasn't much of a hiker, but she was eager to try new experiences. And Dale was such a superb natural athlete that he made her feel safe and confident. On the way up to Oregon, they had stopped to ski in the Sierra Nevada. Neither had ever skied before, and Chantal stuck with the bunny slopes, but after a single day of instruction, Dale whizzed down the expert runs.

Now they followed a winding deer trail to the top of the mountain. It wasn't an easy climb, but the view was worth it—360 degrees of stunning scenery, with the wild ocean crashing below and an emerald green forest stretching toward the east. "It was very romantic," Chantal remembers. "We kissed and held each other close."

When it was time to go back to the car, Dale noticed another trail heading down toward the beach. "This looks like it leads to a different way down," he said. "You want to try it?"

Chantal just smiled and followed his lead. At first it seemed like a great adventure, but suddenly—with painful clarity—they realized they were in trouble. Serious trouble. Over five hundred feet above the beach, the trail became a sheer cliff of loose shale, and a fine rain made the treacherous surface even slicker and softer. When they tried to go back up the way they had come, the shale crumbled wherever they grabbed or stepped. The only direction to go was down.

Dale bravely maintained his confidence. "How's your fear factor?" he asked Chantal. "Do you think we can make it?"

"Let's try," she replied.

Dale led the way, cautiously working his way down, stepping from one small rocky ledge to another, then helping Chantal to follow him—her every movement showering him with loose rocks, mud, and shale. Still almost five hundred feet above the beach, Dale stepped onto a tiny outcrop that looked like the only solid footing, but the rock broke away beneath his weight. He reached back toward Chantal, and for a brief moment, his eyes locked with hers. "He didn't say a word," she recalls. "He knew it was over." Then he fell—smashing his head on a ledge . . . falling . . . falling . . . until Chantal couldn't see him anymore.

"Dale!" she screamed. "Dale! Help! Help!" But there was no answer. Dale was gone, and she was all alone on the cliff. More alone than she had ever been before.

Instinctively, Chantal tried to find a way down—not only to save her own life, but in the desperate hope that Dale was still alive, down on the beach, needing her. It was useless. Every time she moved, the wet shale crumbled away.

Her heart racing with fear and horror, Chantal cried out, "Dear God, please help me!" She hadn't prayed in a long time, but the words came without thinking.

Instantly, she felt a strange, soothing presence "like angels in a mist that came to help me." She heard strange, celestial sounds, "almost music, but not music; maybe the echo of music." Then she began to find her way down the cliff. "I had to make all the moves myself," she explains today, "and I was still living with terror all the way." But before she knew it, and without understanding how it happened, she had descended almost four hundred feet down the sheer, rain-soaked face of the cliff.

Now she was about one hundred feet above the beach. She'd come so far, but there was still a long way to go. She lost her footing and began to slip wildly down the cliff. "Oh no, God, not now!" she cried. At that moment, some awesome force swooped her up "like an invisible hand" and set her firmly back against the rocks. From there she made it down the rest of the way to the beach—though she doesn't remember how.

Safe and alive herself, Chantal found Dale, his beautiful athletic body a broken, lifeless shell. Yet as she gazed upon him, the echo of music grew louder, and she could sense the presence of angels, helping him in his death just as they had helped her in her life. For the first time since the horrible ordeal began, Chantal felt a strange sense of peace. She knelt down and kissed Dale gently on the lips. Then she unfastened the golden necklace he wore around his neck—a perfect match to her own necklace, a symbol of their love.

Numb and shivering in the cold rain, she found a narrow, twisting deer path that led up from the beach, through thick brush, and finally back to the road. A passing motorist took her to the sheriff's office, where they organized a professional rescue party to retrieve Dale's body. But when the rescuers arrived at the top of the cliff—with all their ropes and hooks and special climbing equipment—they realized there was simply no way down. The next morning, they called a helicopter in to land directly on the beach.

Later, one of the rescue team told Chantal, "You're a living, breathing miracle. How you got down that rock face safely is beyond me." Beyond all of us, perhaps.

For many years, Chantal kept her story to herself while she gradually put her life back together—a more spiritual life, with a deeper understanding of God's blessings. Then, several years ago, she married an artist named Andy Lakey, whose life was also changed by an experience with angels. When author Eileen Elias Freeman called Andy to discuss his story, Chantal decided to reveal her own experience, which was included in Freeman's book, *Touched by Angels*. Since then Chantal's story has been told in magazines and on several television shows. Although uncomfortable at first about discussing such a strange and painful memory, she now believes that it is important for the story to be told, so that others will share her sense of peace.

"Ever since the experience," she says today, "I have completely felt the presence of my angels. They have never left me. I feel a real sense of security, and I'm not afraid of dying. I know that the angels are there for us in life, and in death."

WAKE UP!

On New Year's Eve 1971, Michael D. and his wife went to a party on the South Side of Chicago. Their marriage was on the rocks, but they were trying to hang in there and make it work. There were all kinds of problems; for one, they were just too young. At twenty-one, they had already been married for two years, and it hadn't been a whole lot of fun. But there was something else going on as well—something sinister and strange.

In the late '60s, during the height of social protest and political empowerment, Michael had been involved with the Black Panther Party. For various reasons he decided to leave the party, but he had no sooner broken away than he found himself confronted by a man who claimed to be from the FBI. He pressured Michael to turn informer, but when Michael refused, the man told him that the FBI would make his life miserable. Michael believed that the FBI was behind a series of phone calls his wife had received from a woman who claimed to be his girlfriend. These phone calls pushed the already simmering tensions between him and his wife to the boiling point.

At the New Year's Eve party, the couple argued violently and Michael's wife went home alone. When Michael followed her a few hours later, he did what many husbands have done in the midst of a marital argument—he went to sleep on the couch.

Sometime in the early morning darkness of New Year's Day, Michael D. heard a voice in his head saying, "Wake

12

up!" He did as the voice commanded. But though he was fully conscious, he was unable to move, or speak, or open his eyes. The voice had more to say: "Turn over, pretending you're asleep, and take a peek."

Michael had never thought much about spiritual matters. He was more interested in the things of this world. But here he was suddenly confronted with a voice in his head that seemed to have complete control of his body. He decided he'd better do as the voice commanded.

As soon as he accepted the power of the voice, Michael regained control of his body. Very slowly, he turned over on the couch—as if he were rolling in his sleep—and peeked out from under half-closed eyelids. What he saw woke him up in a hurry. His wife was walking toward him with a .30 caliber carbine, calmly inserting a round into the chamber.

Michael reached up from the couch and wrestled the gun away from her. Once he had control of the carbine, he convinced his wife to discuss their differences. They talked until dawn, agreeing to keep working on their relationship.

A couple of weeks later, Michael again heard the voice in his sleep. "Wake up! There's something wrong!"

This time he didn't question the power of the voice. He rose quickly and discovered his wife in the kitchen, standing over the stove boiling a potful of Crisco oil. As Michael wryly explains today, "I didn't exactly see any 'taters out on the counter waiting to be fried."

Michael knew the boiling oil was meant for him. And once again, he convinced his wife to talk about it instead of trying to kill him. Shortly afterwards, he moved out of their apartment.

A few months later, Michael stopped by to discuss some matters with his now-estranged wife. They had a surprisingly pleasant visit, and he ended up spending the night. As he said good-bye the next morning, Michael felt that there was real hope of a reconciliation. But just as he stepped out the back door, he heard his wife calling him back. He walked back through the kitchen and into a long hallway, where he found her waiting with the .30 caliber carbine. She pulled the trigger, and Michael jumped back instinctively, escaping with powder burns across his chest.

Not surprisingly, that was the end of Michael's attempts at reconciliation. Perhaps the most amazing miracle of all is that today he and his ex-wife are good friends who have managed to forgive and forget the violent hatred of the past.

What about the voice that saved Michael's life? Eleven years later, in 1982, Michael D. met the man behind the voice. For that story, see "Who Is This Brother, Anyway?" in August.

ANGELS IN
JOGGING SUITS

IN JANUARY 1989, DENISE SMITH LEFT HER HOME IN
Queens, New York around 5:30 A.M., and made her way
through the dark, icy, deserted streets toward the subway
station. It was the same trip that she made every weekday
morning, the beginning of her commute to downtown Man-
hattan, where she worked as a computer scheduler for a
large company. Most of the production programs and back-
ups ran overnight, so it was important for Denise to get to
work early to check on the overnight processing.

Walking through the icy darkness would be treacherous
for a healthy person, but for Denise, it was almost fool-
hardy. For years, she had suffered from lupus, a chronic
inflammatory disease that can affect many parts of the
body, from skin rashes and joint pain to severe abnormal-
ities of the blood, heart, and lungs. The medication she took
to control the disease, prednisone, had caused severe deterioration of the bones in her knees, so that she could only
walk with the aid of Canadian crutches—the kind that are
braced to the forearms. But that wasn't going to stop Denise. A self-described "tough cookie," she decided that she
was going to make it to work on time, ice or no ice.

Then it happened. As she made her way gingerly down
Jamaica Avenue, past the closed doors of small shops and
the dark windows of second-story apartments, Denise
slipped and fell on the ice—tangled up in her crutches,

unable to move. A large woman to begin with, Denise had grown even larger because of the inactivity caused by her physical problems. That morning, she weighed about 220 pounds, and she simply did not have the strength or mobility in her knees to get up from the sidewalk.

Desperately, Denise looked up and down the street for someone to help her. But there was no one—Jamaica Avenue was absolutely deserted. Although not a particularly religious person, she muttered a quiet prayer to her father, who had died six years earlier. No sooner had she uttered the prayer than she found herself surrounded by five women dressed in jogging suits.

"They picked me up like a feather," Denise recalls, "set me on my feet, told me to be careful, and then ran off. I looked down for a second; then I looked up and they were gone. Again I was alone on the quiet street."

Denise continued to the subway station and made it to work without any further problems. She had never seen the women before, and she has never seen them again. When asked to describe the women, Denise indicated they were "pretty ordinary looking" and that four of them were about her age (mid-thirties), but it's the fifth woman she remembers most clearly.

"I remember mostly the leader. She seemed a little older, maybe in her mid- to late forties. I believe she had short blonde hair. She asked me where I was going and she told me to be careful . . . The strangest thing about the incident was how suddenly those women were there and how suddenly they were gone. They really just seemed to disappear after they ran off."

A few years later, Denise Smith fell on the ice on her way to work in almost the exact same spot. But no "angels" appeared, because she didn't need them. Since the original incident, she has had two successful knee replacements. This time, she got up by herself.

FEBRUARY

The Age of Miracles is forever here!

—THOMAS CARLYLE, 1841

SOMETHING WHITE

The shrine of Lourdes is the most popular site of religious pilgrimage in the world, drawing more visitors than Mecca. But the true story of the events that established the site are not widely known, though they were well-documented by the standards of the time. It all began on a day in February, with an illiterate, asthmatic teenager named Bernadette.

ON THURSDAY, FEBRUARY 11, 1858, FOURTEEN-YEAR-old Bernadette Soubirous walked with her sister and another playmate along the Gave du Pau River, near the town of Lourdes in the mountains of southwestern France. The girls were gathering firewood and bones, which they planned to sell to the local rag-and-bone man. It was a time of famine and hardship in the district, and Bernadette's family—who once owned a mill—had been reduced to extreme poverty.

Some said it was because her father was lazy; others said her mother drank too much. Still others said they were too generous. But whatever the reason, the Soubirous family was now among the poorest citizens of the town, living in a damp, crumbling building that had once been the jail, before the authorities abandoned it as too unhealthy for the prisoners.

Bernadette was the oldest child, a pretty, dark-eyed girl who had suffered from asthma ever since a bout with cholera. When her family lost their mill, she was sent to live with a foster family, but she had recently returned to Lourdes in order to study for her first communion. Although she had a reputation as a sensible young woman, she had trouble learning her catechism. It didn't help that she could neither read nor write.

That morning, the three girls decided to cross a shallow mill stream that ran parallel to the river. They stopped to take off their shoes and socks, just across the stream from a natural rock grotto called Massabielle. But as the others waded the shallow, icy stream, Bernadette lingered behind, afraid that the cold water might set off an asthma attack.

Suddenly she heard a loud rustling like the wind, though she was puzzled that there were no ripples in the stream. The rustling seemed to come from a hedge above the grotto, and when Bernadette looked up she saw the hedge moving and "something white" behind it. She later described the apparition as "a girl in white, no taller than I, who greeted me with a little bow of her head." Bernadette fell to her knees and began to pray. The apparition smiled at her and disappeared into the grotto.

As she came out of her reverie, Bernadette noticed her sister Marie and their friend Jeanne on the other side of the stream—the same side as the grotto. She asked if they had seen anything, and they replied that they had not. They asked her what *she* had seen, and she shrugged it off, saying it was nothing, and continued to gather wood and bones. Later that day, however, she told the other girls about the vision, swearing them both to secrecy. Marie told their mother anyway, and Madame Soubirous beat her two daughters for "telling stories."

Three days later, on Sunday, February 14, Bernadette found herself irresistibly drawn to the grotto. After attending High Mass, she returned accompanied by Marie and several friends, with Jeanne following the little group from a distance. The girls had brought rosaries and a bottle of holy water from the church. As they knelt and prayed, the white figure appeared again, though only Bernadette could see her.

Bernadette sprinkled the apparition with holy water, asking her "to remain if she came from God and go away if not." Just then Jeanne threw a rock from above the grotto, which sent the other girls scurrying away. But Bernadette remained entranced. The girls returned with a local miller, who lifted the visionary in his arms and carried her back to his mill. He later recalled that she was extremely heavy and seemed to be smiling at something he couldn't see.

This incident began to stimulate local interest, and in the early morning of Thursday, February 18—exactly a week after the original apparition—Bernadette returned to the grotto with a prosperous older woman named Madame Millet and the Madame's seamstress. Madame Millet believed that the apparition was a girl named Elisa who had died a few months earlier and was well known for her piety. The older woman gave Bernadette paper, pen, and a writing stand, so that she could ask the figure to write her name. But when Bernadette did so, the apparition replied, "It is not necessary," the first time she had spoken. She then asked Bernadette to come and see her for fifteen consecutive days, saying, "I do not promise to make you happy in this world, but in the next."

Following the instructions of the apparition, Bernadette returned to the grotto and prayed the rosary every day from February 18 to March 4. The "girl in white" appeared to her on all but three of those days, and on the days when she did not appear, Bernadette was led away in tears. During this period, news of the apparition spread throughout the surrounding area, and the crowds that accompanied the teenage visionary grew larger and larger. Although no one except Bernadette saw the figure, many observers were deeply moved by the sight of the dark-eyed girl staring in a trance at something above the grotto.

Disturbed by the growing popular movement, the Lourdes police commissioner stopped Bernadette on Sunday, February 21, and questioned her about her experiences. His report provides the first written account of the events and serves as the basis for much of the story related above. In this first interview, as well as most subsequent interviews, Bernadette didn't identify the figure in white as the Virgin Mary. Instead she referred to it in the local dialect as *aquerò*, which means "that one."

The events took a new turn on February 25. According to Bernadette, *aquerò* told her to "drink from the spring." Not aware of any spring, Bernadette began to walk toward the stream, but *aquerò* called her back and pointed to a spot on the ground. The crowd watched in wonder as the girl knelt down and began to dig with her hands in the dirt, uncovering muddy water and smearing it on her face as she tried to drink it.

Later that day, others dug more deeply on the same spot and did indeed uncover a spring. They took the water back to town, and within days there were reports of miraculous healings from the water. A local pharmacist proclaimed that the water was actually unhealthy, but he later admitted that this was an attempt to discourage the growing popular movement. Almost a century and a half later, this spring still provides the healing water of Lourdes, though modern scientific analysis has found it to be identical to the regular drinking water in the town.

Three days after she uncovered the spring, on February 28, a cousin of Bernadette's father interviewed her in an effort to set down a full account of the miraculous events. When he asked if she had been given a special mission, she replied, "No, not yet." Then on March 2, Bernadette received her mission. For the rest of this story, see "The Chapel, the Shrine, and the Saint" in March.

IF YOUR
DAUGHTER LIVES

A LITTLE AFTER MIDNIGHT ON FEBRUARY 5, 1981, Karen Balik woke up bleeding and vomiting, her body in a state of shock. In the eighth month of pregnancy with her second child, Karen knew immediately that something was horribly wrong. Her husband, Joe, rushed her to the hospital, where she was quickly hooked up to monitors. At first the baby showed no sign of distress, but the placenta had torn, and Karen was wheeled into surgery for an emergency C-section.

The next thing Karen remembers is waking up in the recovery room in terrible pain. Joe wasn't there. A female doctor wearing East Indian dress leaned over her and delivered the bad news in blunt, no-nonsense terms: "If your daughter lives, she will have many problems. Her lungs collapsed twice and it took ten minutes to revive her. She will be brain damaged and maybe deaf, blind or retarded."

"I wanted to scream," Karen remembers today, "but my stomach hurt so bad! I couldn't believe my husband wasn't there when I was told."

At the time his wife was facing a mother's nightmare, Joe was still in the waiting room; no one had bothered to inform him that his wife was out of surgery. Usually a polite and mild-mannered sort of guy, Joe Balik had plenty to say about the way the doctor had delivered the bad news

23

to his wife. But the doctor's poor bedside manner didn't change the medical reality. The baby had gone without oxygen for ten minutes, considered the outer limit of human survival. More than five minutes without oxygen usually produces permanent brain damage, and babies who survive ten minutes invariably suffer from cerebral palsy or other severe developmental disorders.

The baby was immediately placed on a respirator. One of her heart valves wouldn't open, and the doctors didn't know if she'd ever be able to breathe without the respirator. The veins in her arms collapsed from so many IVs, and they had to start inserting the IVs into the veins of her head. She was fed through a tube in her nose. And of course, there were the dire predictions of severe developmental problems.

"I held her every day," Karen recalls, "and when I went back to my room, I would cry while every mother was holding their healthy baby. I wondered what she would be like since they gave me no hope."

While the medical staff at the neonatal unit bluntly prepared them for the worst, Joe and Karen turned to their faith in God. They had the baby baptized immediately, using the name "Mary," a custom that many Catholics follow when they are not sure if a baby girl will survive. Both of their families united in prayer, but Joe's mother, Josephine, approached the crisis with a special fervor. Always a deeply religious person, Josephine made the survival of her grandchild her own spiritual responsibility, crying out to the original Mary, patroness of Mothers—and grandmothers—everywhere.

"Dear Blessed Mother," she prayed, "if you answer my prayer to save our baby's life—and let the doctors be wrong in their diagnosis—I promise I will go to Mass every day for the rest of my life, as long as my legs will carry me." She went to Mass every day, praying fervently that God would spare this little one and give her a chance to grow up in the beautiful world that He had made for his children.

After a week, the doctors tried taking the baby off the respirator. This was the moment of truth, for if she stayed too long on the machine, she might never learn to breathe on her own. But she did breathe—all by herself—with the lungs that God had given her. It was the beginning of a long, hard climb toward a healthy life. As her grandmother Josephine continued to pray and attend Mass each day, the baby grew stronger and stronger until finally, five weeks after her traumatic birth, Joe and Karen took their daughter home for the first time. Now that they believed she would live, her name was changed to Heather Mary.

There were still complications. At the age of three months, Heather developed water on the brain as a result of the traumatic birth. A thin tube called a shunt was implanted under her skin to drain the fluid from the brain back into the perineal cavity, where it is metabolized by the body. When the shunt collapsed a week later, replacement surgery was required. She also required hernia surgery while still an infant, and a new shunt at the age of five.

Despite her rough start, Heather Mary Balik is now a happy, active eighth-grader. She wears glasses and takes some special education classes, but her intelligence level is normal and she does just fine in regular classes by working a little harder. Heather comes by that attitude naturally, for she's been a fighter since the beginning—with help from a loving family and a very special grandmother who believed that God and the Blessed Mother could offer joy where medical science offered only sorrow.

"She is bright, reliable, and has a spirit that never gives up," her mother writes. "The teachers love her because she never stops trying, and is a role model to all the children. The parents in the neighborhood keep her busy babysitting their children. She never gave up, and she beat all the odds. . . . That is our miracle: Heather Mary Balik!"

SAVED BY
THE STORM

Sometimes miracles happen in ways we would never imagine. Take the following tale of strange good fortune that touched the family of my wife's great-grandfather during the Great Depression.

LOUIS FISHER WAS A SCRAP-IRON DEALER IN CHICAGO during the glorious days of the Roaring Twenties. It was the age of Al Capone and Bugsy Moran, when crooks made millions selling illegal liquor and otherwise-upright citizens partied the night away in illegal clubs called speakeasies. But there was plenty of honest money to be made as well, and Louis made a comfortable living buying and selling used metal.

During the early twenties, the Fisher family moved into a home on Edgemont Avenue, just southwest of downtown. Today, Edgemont is called Grenshaw—a run-down street near the concrete Chicago campus of the University of Illinois. But in those days it was a pleasant neighborhood of solid middle-class families. Built in the nineteenth century, none of the houses on Edgemont had electricity or indoor plumbing—until the Fishers moved in and installed both.

For a few sweet years, the family enjoyed their life and their home. Louis's wife, Mary, wore the latest fashions and fine jewelry, while the older Fisher children attended college. Then suddenly tragedy struck. At the age of fifty, in the prime of his life, Louis Fisher died of cancer.

Mary and her two oldest sons did their best to keep the family afloat. But when the Stock Market crashed and the Great Depression grabbed America by the throat, the Fishers suffered along with the rest of the nation. Mary had to pawn her jewels to pay off the medical bills from Louis's long illness, and there wasn't much left to live on.

At the same time, the Edgemont Avenue neighborhood began to decline. Houses didn't sell and landlords couldn't rent. When people couldn't pay their mortgage, banks repossessed their homes. But the banks couldn't sell them either. More and more houses on the street were abandoned. Finally, the Fishers abandoned their house. They didn't bother to try and sell it. They just moved away.

The family settled in a nicer neighborhood on the West Side and began to put their lives back together. Then one day, they received an official letter from the city of Chicago informing them that the house on Edgemont Avenue had been condemned and that it was their responsibility to pay for demolition. The letter further informed them that until the house was torn down, they would be liable for any injuries that might occur because of the house's hazardous condition.

In the early thirties—the darkest days of the Depression—it seemed impossible that the Fishers would ever find the money to pay for the demolition of their house on Edgemont Avenue. A deeply religious woman, Mary Fisher cried, and prayed, and hoped for a miracle. "Please God," she whispered, "lift this burden from us."

That winter, a powerful storm swept down from the north and hit the city of Chicago with all its frozen fury. Snow, driven by a relentless howling wind, piled on rooftops and drifted over first-floor windows. Even for people who were accustomed to winter storms, it seemed like a storm to end all storms. The entire city was at a standstill.

Finally the storm ended, and the people of Chicago began to go out again into the streets. The Fishers decided to take a look at their house on Edgemont Avenue, to see just what needed to be done. But when they returned to their old neighborhood, they discovered that the storm had already done the job for them. The house had been demolished right to the ground! All they had to do was pick up the pieces and cart them away.

OUT OF THE AIR

For centuries, reports of the wondrous powers of Indian holy men have filtered into the West. Although these reports are intriguing, it's difficult for skeptical westerners to accept them without some sort of objective documentation. During the early 1970s, two psychic researchers traveled to India to examine some of these reports and returned with surprising results.

Karlis Osis of the American Society of Psychical Research and Erlendur Haraldsson of the University of Iceland made two trips to India in the early 1970s, hoping to convince the famous, holy man, Sri Sathya Sai Baba, to submit his powers to tests under laboratory conditions. At that time, Baba was in his late forties, and he had exhibited remarkable powers ever since childhood. The most common miracle ascribed to him—if a miracle can be called common—is the materialization of objects out of the air. Baba's followers have reported witnessing materializations of everything from religious medals and a sacred ash called *vibuti* to fruits and vegetables out of season and hot food in a moving car.

Osis and Haraldsson met with Baba several times at his ashram in southern India. At that time he refused to submit to scientific experiments, saying that he would use his powers only for religious purposes, as a means of strengthening the spiritual faith of his followers. But even as he argued

29

back and forth with his western visitors over the laboratory experiments, he demonstrated the very powers they wanted to measure, under conditions that were not that far removed from those of a laboratory.

In a paper presented at the 18th Annual Convention of the Parapsychological Association in 1975, Osis and Haraldsson reported that they observed "at close range" fourteen different instances of appearances or disappearances of objects. Two incidents in particular seem truly miraculous, especially when we consider that the witnesses did not come to Sai Baba as believers or devotees, but rather as skeptical, western-educated researchers who were there solely to observe and analyze the holy man. Both these incidents occurred in Sai Baba's interview room, which the researchers described as "bare with concrete walls and floor and no carpets. The only furniture in the room was one armchair . . . we all sat cross-legged on the floor."

During an argument about the question of experiments, Sai Baba explained that the spiritual life and the daily life should be grown together like a "double *rudraksha*." The visitors didn't understand the term, and the translator was unable to clarify it. Sai Baba struggled for some time to explain what he meant until, with an agitation that the westerners interpreted as impatience, he closed his fist, waved his hand, and opened his palm to reveal a double *rudraksha*: a type of nut that in rare instances grows two together as one, just as we sometimes see a double apple or, more commonly, a double cherry.

After the visitors had examined the double *rudraksha*, Sai Baba said he wanted to give it as a present to Erlendur Haraldsson. He then wrapped both hands around the nut, blew on it, and opened his hands to offer the gift. To their amazement, the researchers saw that the *rudraksha* now had a golden ornamented shield on each side and a golden cross with a ruby attached to it.

Sleight of hand? Perhaps, but Osis and Haraldsson didn't think so. "Sai Baba wears a one-piece gown-like dress with sleeves that reach his wrists," they reported. "We observed his hands very closely and could not see him take anything from his sleeves or reach toward his bushy hair, clothes or any other hiding place." Later, the researchers examined one of Baba's gowns and found no hidden pockets or other possible hiding places. They discussed the issue with another pair of western researchers who had examined a gown with similar results. And they point out that some of the objects Sai Baba has materialized—such as ash or food—leave his hands dirty or greasy but no one has ever seen any evidence of this on his gowns.

On another occasion, Osis and Haraldsson witnessed a miraculous demonstration that was almost the exact opposite of the first event. Once again, the context was an argument between Sai Baba and his western visitors over the importance of controlled experiments. And once again the object involved was a gift from the holy man to the researchers—in this case a golden ring that Baba had given to Karlis Osis. An enameled color picture of Sai Baba was set into the ring like a precious stone. The "stone" was held in place, first by a frame with four small notches protruding over the stone, and then by the ring itself, with edges above and below the frame and the stone.

During the course of the argument, Sai Baba again appeared impatient with the discussion and said to Karlis Osis, "Look at your ring." When Osis did so, he was astounded to discover that the stone had completely disappeared. The ring showed no sign of damage or tampering. The frame that had surrounded the stone was still in place, and the four notches that had protruded over the stone were not bent.

"When Sai Baba made us aware of the stone's absence," the researchers reported, "we were sitting cross-legged on the floor several feet away from him. We had not shaken hands when we entered and he did not reach out to us or touch us. K. O. [Karlis Osis] had his hands placed on his thighs and E. H. [Erlendur Haraldsson] had noticed the stone in the ring during this sitting just before this incident."

When the western visitors were unable to find the stone,

Sai Baba wryly commented, "This was my experiment."

Osis and Haraldsson also investigated reports of out-of-body experiences by Indian holy men. For that story, see "Out of Body" in April.

MARCH

How does he work such miracles?

—THE GOSPEL OF MARK

LORD, WHATEVER
THE OUTCOME

On Saturday, March 28, 1987, a baby girl was born in Laurel, Mississippi. She was named Ashley, and she was the first-born child of her parents, Mike and Jan. Normally, it would have been a moment of boundless joy. But there wasn't anything "normal" about Ashley's birth. Born eight weeks premature, she came into the world with no heartbeat and no respiration. The medical staff at the hospital in Laurel resuscitated her, hooked her up to life support, and rushed her by ambulance to a neonatal intensive care unit at a hospital in the capital city of Jackson, almost one hundred miles away.

Jan had lost a great deal of blood during the emergency C-section, so Mike stayed with her at the hospital in Laurel, while his parents followed Ashley to Jackson. Mike and Jan prayed for their daughter and asked their families and the members of their church to pray as well, but the first days of little Ashley's life were enough to test the faith of any parent. For Mike it was even more difficult; as director of psychology at a residential treatment center for handicapped children, he saw children every day who suffered the effects of birth trauma: mental retardation, autism, cerebral palsy. He couldn't help thinking of the difficult life that awaited his daughter—if she ever had a life at all.

At 6:00 A.M. on Monday, March 30, Mike was in Jan's hospital room when he received a call from one of the neonatal doctors in Jackson. They had been working with Ashley for several hours, he said, and she was not responding. Her left lung was completely blocked, and she was breathing off her right lung with the ventilator providing one hundred percent oxygen at the highest possible pressure. If her condition didn't change, the doctor warned, they would lose her.

Mike's parents had assured him that the neonatal ICU in Jackson was first-rate, and the medical team there was doing everything "humanly possible" to save Ashley. But now it seemed that humanly possible wasn't enough. Mike and Jan prayed again, and as friends and family arrived that morning, they added their prayers. Although he appreciated the concern of the visitors, Mike felt a need to be alone for awhile. So he went to his parents' house, to the bedroom that had been his as a child. There he knelt and prayed and cried. And the prayer he spoke through his tears was the prayer of a man with a deep, abiding faith. "I know you can heal my baby," he said, "but if you don't and she dies, I will still serve you and my faith will still grow. Lord, whatever the outcome, it is well with my soul."

"Immediately, in my spirit," Mike remembers today, "the Lord said, 'All is well,' and the deepest peace settled over me, and all I could do was weep. I looked at my watch and it was nine-fifteen."

Feeling an enormous sense of relief, Mike showered and dressed and returned to the hospital, where he told his wife and family what had happened. He felt so convinced that his daughter had been healed that he had not yet called the neonatal unit to check on her. But now he made the call, and the peace he felt in his heart and spirit was confirmed.

"She's like a different baby," the nurse told him. "Her blood gasses are normal, she is resting, and from all indications both lungs are open and functioning normally."

When Mike asked at what time the change had occurred, the nurse replied that it had been at a little after nine.

That afternoon, Mike drove to Jackson to see Ashley for the first time since her birth. She was so tiny, still connected to the respirator and the other equipment. But she was awake and aware. She was going to live.

Although he was awestruck by this clear display of God's healing power, Mike still had moments of doubt and darkness. Three days later, when he brought his wife home from the hospital, he sat in his living room, thinking about all the terrible problems that might still await Ashley because of her traumatic birth. At that very moment, a co-worker called. She said she had been praying for him that Monday morning—around the same time that Ashley had shown such remarkable improvement—and she wanted to pass along some verses from the Bible for inspiration. She told him to write the verses down and read them whenever he felt doubt or fear.

Mike did as his friend suggested, turning to his Bible and copying out the verses. Two of the passages—one from the Book of Isaiah, the other from the Gospel of John—were quite clear to him, for they both emphasized the awesome power that God works in our lives. But the third passage, from the Book of Daniel, puzzled him. It was the reply of three Israelites to King Nebuchadnezzar, who threatened to throw them into a fiery furnace unless they worshipped his god and bowed down before his golden idol:

> If it be so, our God whom we serve is able to deliver us from the burning fiery furnace, and he will deliver us out of thine hand, O king.
> But if not, be it known unto thee, O king, that we will not serve thy gods, nor worship the golden image which thou hast set up.

Mike read the passage over and over, trying to understand how this applied to his own situation. Finally it became clear. He had prayed in the spirit of the Israelites, affirming his faith in God whatever the outcome of his prayer. He tucked the verses into his wallet and carried them with him for months, taking them out to read whenever he felt a moment of doubt.

Ashley came home at the age of five weeks, when her weight had reached four and a half pounds. Although the doctors told them not to expect too much of her as she grew up, Mike and Jan placed their faith in the healing power of God. And that faith was rewarded. Today, almost nine years later, Ashley is a healthy third-grader in the gifted program at school. As Mike writes joyfully, "All is well. We serve a mighty God."

IN TWO WEEKS
IT WILL BE GONE

IN THE WORLD OF BUSINESS, JEAN WAS AN UNEQUIVOCAL success. Attractive, creative, and highly-educated, she was an expert in communication and public relations. She'd produced educational videos on subjects ranging from nutrition to passing the SAT and coordinated training workshops for a wide variety of corporate clients. She had even served as the director of her local chamber of commerce.

When it came to romance, however, Jean was less fortunate. She was involved with a married man, and though he promised to leave his wife and marry Jean, several years had passed and the promise still hovered between them as nothing more than empty words.

Overall, Jean was in excellent health. She ate right and got plenty of exercise. In fact, she was so trim and energetic that most people assumed she was ten years younger than her real age—and Jean didn't bother to set them straight. Her only health problem in recent years had occurred in 1985, when she had an ovarian cyst surgically removed. But the surgery had gone smoothly, and that was all in the past—at least that's what Jean thought.

Then, in 1988, Jean felt a strangely familiar pain and cramping. She made an appointment at the Scripps Clinic in La Jolla, California, where a physician confirmed Jean's suspicions. It was another ovarian cyst. The doctor recommended surgery.

Although Jean respected traditional medicine, she also had a strong interest in alternative forms of healing. For years she had been encouraging other people to get in touch with their thoughts and feelings, to understand the emotional context of their physical problems. But when it came to her own problems, she reverted to a less enlightened point of view. Now she decided to practice what she preached.

"No surgery," she told the doctor. "In two weeks, when I come back, it'll be gone."

The doctor just smiled and wished her luck.

At the time she developed the cyst, Jean was already seeing a massage therapist, whom she considered a very special and talented person. Their early sessions had focused on the physical body, but now she asked the therapist to help her work through her emotions along with the physical massage. Jean believed that the location and nature of a disease had significance. Why the ovaries? Why a cyst? "I just decided to let myself discover what it was all about," she remembers.

Gradually the situation became clear. Jean realized that she was extremely angry at her married lover. She felt that he was using her sexually and stringing her along with his promise to leave his wife, a promise he evidently had no intention of keeping. "It was like a bubble of rage in my body," she recalls. And the bubble of rage became the cyst—a cyst on her ovaries so she could not have sex with her lover.

Once she identified the source of the problem, Jean was ready to heal under the skilled hands of her massage therapist. "As he worked on the area," she recalls, "I could actually feel the bubble of rage dissolving."

Two weeks after her initial appointment, Jean returned to the Scripps Clinic. The young doctor examined her carefully, searching for the cyst. But it was gone. Completely.

"The doctor just smiled and gave me a big hug," Jean remembers.

Today, Jean has her own healing practice, helping clients work through their problems. She firmly believes that we can create our own miracles. "The physical disease is often just an encapsulation of an underlying emotional problem," she explains. "If you can get through to the emotional context, you can heal the physical disease."

THE CHAPEL,
THE SHRINE, AND
THE SAINT

In February 1858, fourteen-year-old Bernadette Soubirous saw a series of apparitions in a grotto near Lourdes, France. The first part of Bernadette's story is told in "Something White" in February. The month of March brought a new, startling revelation that led to the Lourdes we know today.

On March 2, 1858, Bernadette Soubirous went to the grotto just as she had done every day since February 18—when the mysterious figure in white had asked her to come for fifteen consecutive days. This was the thirteenth day of the period, and the excitement over the apparitions had spread throughout the region. Some 1,600 spectators accompanied Bernadette that day.

Bernadette called the apparition *aquerò*, a word in the local dialect that means "that one." Up to this time *aquerò* had promised Bernadette happiness in the next world, and she had indicated a spot on the ground where Bernadette dug and discovered a spring—a spring whose waters were already being credited with healing properties. But she had not stated her name or explained the purpose of the apparitions.

On this morning, Bernadette did as she always did; she knelt on the ground before the grotto and began to say the rosary. When *aquerò* appeared, she told Bernadette to go to the priests and tell them to build a chapel on the site, so that people could go there in procession. Bernadette went directly to the rectory in Lourdes with two of her aunts, and tried to relay the message to the curé (pastor) of the parish, Abbé Peyramale. But the priest didn't want to hear about it. He called her a liar and complained that her family caused nothing but trouble. It didn't help that both of Bernadette's aunts had gotten pregnant out of wedlock.

Peyramale ushered them out so quickly that she never had a chance to say anything about the chapel. That evening the teenager returned to try again. None of her family was willing to go with her, so she went with a sister of her father's employer. This time there were other priests present as well, and she received a more polite response. Abbé Peyramale told Bernadette to ask *aquerò* her name and to request that she make the rose bush in the grotto bloom. Apparently by this time, *aquerò* had come to be identified with the Virgin Mary, and the blooming rose bush was considered a sign that only Mary could provide. The following day, Bernadette relayed the request, but *aquerò* just smiled and asked again that a chapel be built on the site.

On March 4, the last day of the fifteen-day period, a crowd of around 8,000 people came to the grotto. The atmosphere was half carnival and half religious expectation. But there were no great signs and wonders. Bernadette simply did what she always did. In *Encountering Mary,* religious scholar Sandra L. Zimdars-Swartz describes the actions of the young visionary: ". . . she knelt, lit her candle, began to pray the rosary, stopped praying for a time while staring at a spot above the grotto, then resumed the rosary, blew out her candle, rose, and departed." When later asked what had happened, Bernadette replied that *aquerò* had not spoken because she was angry with the crowd's lack of faith.

As she walked away from the grotto, Bernadette embraced a sick girl named Eugénie Troy, who wore a cloth over her sensitive eyes to protect them from the sun. Rumors quickly circulated that the child had been healed of blindness, the first of several healings attributed to Bernadette at this time. In the weeks that followed, hundreds of people came to see her, bringing gifts and offering money. Bernadette refused all these gifts and offerings, and denied that she had healed Eugénie Troy or anyone else. Considering her age and the dire poverty of her family, she maintained an impressive integrity and level-headedness during the entire series of apparitions.

Bernadette stayed away from the grotto for three weeks after the disappointment of March 4. She returned on March 25, the Feast of the Annunciation, which commemorates the day that the angel Gabriel announced to Mary that she would have a son by the Holy Spirit. That morning, Bernadette went very early, accompanied by perhaps twenty to one hundred people—a far cry from the raucous multitudes of her previous visit. The spectators saw what they always saw: a dark-eyed girl praying the rosary and staring in a trance at a spot above the grotto. However, afterwards Bernadette reported a startling piece of news. *Aquerò* had finally revealed her name, saying "I am the Immaculate Conception."

This revelation proved a major turning point in the story of Lourdes. The doctrine of the Immaculate Conception—the Catholic belief that Mary was born without the taint of Original Sin—had only been proclaimed as official doctrine four years earlier. Bernadette didn't understand the words and had to keep repeating them to herself all the way to the rectory, where she reported them to the ever-doubting Abbé Peyramale. The priest responded negatively at first, though it's unclear whether he was astounded or angry. However, he soon changed his attitude and became Bernadette's staunch supporter and protector.

In truth, from this moment on, it was Abbé Peyramale who spearheaded the religious movement at Lourdes rather than Bernadette Soubirous. Peyramale was better educated than most rural priests of the time, and as he considered Bernadette's latest revelation, he must have seen its deeper significance for his own parish and for the entire Catholic Church. The Immaculate Conception was a relatively new and—from an objective point of view—rather strange doctrine, and here was a message from heaven affirming that doctrine.

It was not until July that Peyramale was able to convince the local bishop to launch an official investigation. In the meantime, the popular movement exploded into mass hysteria. Other young people hopped on the spiritual bandwagon, claiming visions of their own and attracting followers. During June of 1858, local police officials barricaded the grotto, only to have the barricades torn down three times by believers, until the bishop ordered the barricades to remain. In October, the barricades were permanently removed by order of Emperor Napoleon III, who believed his two-year-old son had been cured of sunstroke by the waters.

Bernadette told her story twice to the bishop's commission, and in both cases, the illiterate teenager deeply impressed the investigators with her simple honesty and integrity. In January 1862, Bishop Laurence of Tarbes officially sanctioned the worship of "Mary Immaculate, Mother of God" at the grotto and declared seven reported miraculous healings to be genuine. That year, construction began on a church, and four years later the railroad built tracks to Lourdes, bringing pilgrims from throughout France, and ultimately from throughout the world.

Today, some four million pilgrims visit Lourdes each year. Two more churches have been built, including an underground basilica that holds 20,000 people, the second largest church in the world. An independent group of doctors, formed in 1882, investigates every reported cure, subjecting it to rigorous medical evaluation, including a physical examination immediately after the cure and a follow-up examination a year later. Out of more than 5,000 reported cures, the church has pronounced over sixty to be miraculous, and there are hundreds of other cases that seem equally remarkable.

And what of Bernadette, the dark-eyed teenager who

started it all? While others made wild-eyed claims of visions, Bernadette saw *aquerò* only two more times, on April 7 and July 16. She remained aloof from the growing hysteria, and in May 1858—amid reports of miraculous healings from the spring that she had uncovered—Bernadette herself went to a nearby town to take their waters for her asthma. In June she finally made her first communion, but Abbé Peyramale had to fight off an effort to commit the young visionary to an insane asylum. To further protect her, Peyramale arranged for her to live at the school she attended in Lourdes, run by the Sisters of Charity. In 1866, the same year the railroad arrived in Lourdes, Bernadette moved to the motherhouse of the order in the distant town of Nevers and spent the rest of her life there as a nun.

Always a sickly young woman, she developed a reputation among her fellow sisters for suffering her illnesses with extraordinary good humor and humility. Once, when another nun brought up the subject of the apparitions at Lourdes, Bernadette rhetorically asked what she did with a broom when she was finished sweeping. "You put it behind a door, and that is what the Virgin has done with me. While I was useful she used me, and now she has put me behind the door."

Bernadette died on April 16, 1879, at the age of thirty-five, of tuberculosis and other maladies that made her last years agony. Several miraculous cures had been attributed to her during her life, and reports of miracles increased after her death. In 1909, in a ritual on the path to Catholic sainthood, her body was exhumed and found to be remarkably incorrupt; even the habit in which she was buried remained intact—thirty years after her death.

An incorruptible body is among the traditional signs of sanctity recognized by the Church. But even the official inspirational literature readily admits it is "not necessarily miraculous." The literature goes on to explain that a corpse decays at a slower rate—and may even mummify—depending upon the nature of the soil and the humidity. At the same time, the literature continues, the perfect state of Bernadette's body "is quite astounding," because of her illnesses and the humidity in the vault where she was buried. After the medical examination, the nuns washed their former sister's corpse and reburied it in a new casket. Even as they closed the lid they noticed that her face had begun to turn black from exposure to the air.

The perfect state of Bernadette's body became a sort of morbid fascination. It was exhumed and examined two more times, in 1919 and 1925, when it was finally placed in an ornate casket of glass and gold. By then, due to exposure to the air, the normal process of decomposition had begun. A company in Paris made a wax death mask to lay over her face, and the body was displayed at the chapel convent in Nevers, where it remains today as a popular place of pilgrimage on the way home from Lourdes. Bernadette was canonized by the Catholic Church on December 8, 1933, the Feast of the Immaculate Conception.

The story of one remarkable cure at Lourdes is told in "A Miracle in the Grotto" in July.

A YOGI IN LIFE
AND DEATH

Incorruptibility of the body after death is not limited to Catholic saints. Here's a modern story from the Hindu tradition.

PARAMAHANSA YOGANANDA CAME TO AMERICA IN 1920, bringing with him the sacred Indian teachings of kriya yoga. Long before eastern religion and philosophy became fashionable, Yogananda worked tirelessly to unite East and West in a vision of spiritual brotherhood. Along with yogic teachings, he respectfully presented the teachings of other holy people, including Jesus, Moses, Mohammed, and Buddha. Yogananda saw no conflict among the great religions of the world.

In his life story, *Autobiography of a Yogi,* Yogananda described many extraordinary miracles that he had witnessed in India. But perhaps the most striking miracle—at least to those of us in the West—is the miracle that occurred after he passed from this world in Los Angeles on March 7, 1952.

To a yogic master, the end of this life is not considered death, but rather the final conscious exit from the body, called *mahasamadhi*. For months, Yogananda had hinted to his followers that his time on earth was drawing short. "I have a very important engagement in March," he would

48

say. But when his disciples asked him to be more specific, he would look away in spiritual detachment. It was only in retrospect that they realized all his activities during the final days of his life followed a clear and careful plan of preparation for the end.

On the evening of March 7, Yogananda—the spiritual ambassador—attended a banquet honoring the Indian ambassador to the United States, a fitting exit for a man who had worked all his life to bring East and West together. Photographs taken at the banquet show him in apparent good health, smiling serenely, his eyes already focused on the next world. After several other speakers, Yogananda stepped to the podium and briefly addressed his favorite themes of peace and unity. "India has great things to give to you," he said, "and America can very greatly help India. . . . Let us work for peace on earth as never before. We want a congress of scientists, of ambassadors, of religious men who will constantly think how to make this world a better home, a spiritual home with God as our Guide."

Yogananda closed his speech with a few lines from a poem he had written about his native India, a place where "men dream God." Then, with a beautiful smile on his face, he simply slid to the floor and entered *mahasamadhi*. The official medical diagnosis was a heart attack, but no one who saw him pass on observed anything but grace, peace, and spiritual joy.

The body was taken to Yogananda's home in the Los Angeles neighborhood of Mount Washington. The following evening, after his close friends and followers had paid their private respects, it was transported to the famous Forest Lawn Memorial-Park in nearby Glendale, where the mortuary staff noted that "it presented no signs of physical deterioration and no putrefactive odor—two very unusual absences when a death has occurred twenty-four hours earlier."

Since Yogananda's followers planned several more days of viewing, the morticians carried out minimal embalming procedures in the interests of public health. However, they decided that normal cosmetic procedures were "superfluous,'' because there were no visible changes to the skin. The body was then returned to the Mount Washington headquarters of the Self Realization Fellowship, the organization Yogananda had founded to spread his teachings. After the final rites on March 11, the glass sealer lid of the bronze coffin was fastened securely, and the body was never touched again by human hands.

Up to this point, the perfect condition of Yogananda's body was already remarkable enough to garner the attention of the experienced mortuary staff at Forest Lawn. But the events of the next two weeks were even more remarkable. Officers of the Self Realization Fellowship believed that two of the yogi's disciples might arrive from India sometime in March, so they requested that Forest Lawn keep the body under daily observation, in hopes that the disciples might be able to view the form of their beloved teacher. The mortuary director, Harry T. Rowe, attested to the amazing results of this observation.

> At the time of receiving Paramahansa Yogananda's body, the mortuary personnel at Forest Lawn expected to observe, through the glass lid of the casket, the usual progressive signs of bodily decay. Our astonishment increased as day followed day without bringing any visible change in the body under observation. Paramahansa Yogananda's body was apparently in a phenomenal state of immutability.

On March 27, twenty days after Yogananda's death, Fellowship officers ordered the casket permanently closed, because they had received word that the disciples would not be arriving from India. The glass inner lid was sealed to the coffin by fire, and the heavy bronze outer cover was bolted into place. "The physical appearance of Yogananda on March twenty-seventh just before the bronze cover of the casket was put into position, was the same as it had been on March seventh," Rowe reported. "He looked on March twenty-seventh as fresh and unravaged by decay as he had looked on the night of his death."

Interestingly, Yogananda's followers were unaware of

the miracle-in-progress, since they communicated with the
Forest Lawn administration rather than the mortuary staff.
The story only came to light some six weeks later, and
Harry Rowe agreed to present a full, detailed account in a
notarized letter for publication in the Fellowship magazine.
This in itself seems impressive, because the western attitude
toward non-Christian religions was less tolerant in the
1950s than it is today. But Rowe was genuinely astounded
by what he had observed, and he gladly presented his account "in the interests of truth."

"The absence of any visual signs of decay in the dead
body of Paramahansa Yogananda offers the most extraordinary case in our experience," he wrote. ". . . No odor of
decay emanated from [his] body at any time . . . no indication of mold was visible on [his] skin, and no visible
desiccation (drying up) took place in the bodily tissues.
This state of perfect preservation of a body is, so far as we
know from mortuary annals, an unparalleled one."

Throughout the centuries, there have been many stories
of holy people whose bodies appeared as fresh and healthy
in death as they had in life. But the miraculous incorruptibility of Yogananda's body occurred in the modern age,
in a modern city, and was sworn to by the director of a
world-famous, modern mortuary. It was the final miracle of
Paramahansa Yogananda's miraculous life.

APRIL

All creation is governed by law . . . The principles that operate in the outer universe, discoverable by scientists, are called natural laws. But there are subtler laws that rule the hidden spiritual planes and the inner realm of consciousness . . .

—AUTOBIOGRAPHY OF A YOGI

OUR LADY OF EGYPT

On the night of April 2, 1968, three Moslem auto mechanics were working in a shop in Zeitoun, Egypt, a lower-class suburb of Cairo. They decided to step outside for some fresh air, and immediately noticed a strange, glowing form on the roof of a Coptic Christian church across the street. Thinking that it was a woman who was about to jump, one of the men called the emergency rescue squad while another went to get the pastor of the church. In the meantime—drawn by the brilliant light—a small crowd gathered on the street. Although the light was too dazzling to identify facial features, some of the onlookers identified the figure as Mary, the mother of Jesus, and when they called out praise in Mary's name, the figure seemed to acknowledge them with a bow. Then it ascended into the dark sky and disappeared.

Rumors quickly circulated throughout the Cairo area that Mary had appeared on the roof of the church. The rumors were not surprising, because—although Zeitoun is primarily Moslem—there is a strong local tradition related to Mary. It's believed that the Holy Family came to Zeitoun during their flight to Egypt, described in the New Testament. More recently, in 1925, the church itself had been built with funds donated by a local family, after a family member had dreams in which Mary promised to appear if they would build a church for her. The church was named St. Mary's.

What happened on the nights following the apparition,

however, was very surprising. The figure continued to appear frequently—not every night, but often enough to draw huge crowds to the quiet street, so huge that the city government had to tear down several old buildings to make room for them. During the next fourteen months, there were over seventy apparitions witnessed by between 250,000 to 500,000 people. Crowds averaged around 10,000 each night, and on those nights when the apparition lasted long enough for people to call their friends, as many as 100,000 people gathered outside the church. They included Moslems, Coptic Christians, Roman Catholics, and Protestants; Egyptians, Greeks, and Americans; men and women, adults and children, believers and nonbelievers.

Unlike many apparitions, what these people saw did not seem to depend on what they believed. Although there are slight differences in eyewitness descriptions, they all agree on the essential fact: a luminous, white or bluish-white figure, dressed in flowing robes of light and with a glowing halo around its head, appeared on the roof of the church, often walking around the dome and raising her hands as if to bless the crowd. Many also saw sparks of lights that some called stars, but most called doves. These doves of light often accompanied the figure, but also appeared alone. On some nights when the figure did not appear, observers reported that the whole dome glowed, as if it were melting in the light or enveloped in a smoky fog.

One of the auto mechanics who originally saw the figure had been scheduled to have a gangrenous finger amputated the very next morning, but when he arrived at the hospital, the doctors discovered that the finger had completely healed, and the surgery was canceled. This was the first of several hundred spontaneous cures reported in the Zeitoun area. In August of 1968, the Coptic Church formed a medical commission to investigate the cures, and many were found to be inexplicable by natural healing processes.

The Egyptian government also launched an official investigation into the apparitions and declared it an "undeniable fact" that Mary had appeared to both Christians and Moslems. This pan-religious response is one of the most amazing aspects of the apparitions, for the Christian minority of Egypt has weathered centuries of acrimony and religious restriction at the hands of the Moslem majority. Yet here they were praying together side-by-side before the luminous lady. As writer Victor DeVincenzo points out in his historical overview of the phenomena, "It was the first time that anyone could remember Moslems and Christians worshipping together in Egypt."

Two of the best eyewitness accounts come from officials of the Coptic Church who investigated the apparition in April. The Coptic Church broke off from the Orthodox Church in the fifth century, and is ruled by its own pope and its own hierarchy of bishops. One of the church officials, Bishop Samuel described the apparition as follows:

> At 2:45 in the morning the Blessed Virgin Mary appeared in a complete luminous body as a radiant phosphorescent statue. After a short while the apparition vanished. It reappeared at four o'clock and remained until five o'clock—dawn. The scene was overwhelming and magnificent. The apparition walked toward the west, sometimes moving its hands in blessing, and sometimes bowing repeatedly. A halo of light surrounded its head. I saw some glittering beings around the apparition. They looked like stars, rather blue in color. . . .

Another Coptic official, Bishop Athanasius, used almost the same words to describe the apparition:

> There she was, five or six meters above the dome, high in the sky, full figure, like a phosphorous statue, but not so stiff as a statue. . . . Our Lady looked to the north; she waved her hand; she blessed the people, sometimes in the direction where we stood. Her garments swayed in the wind. She was very quiet, full of glory. It was something really supernatural, very, very heavenly.

Although the testimony of the Coptic bishops was particularly eloquent, there are similar descriptions by those with no official connection to the church. Michael Takla, editor of the Egyptian periodical *Watani* witnessed the apparitions on several occasions and summed them up as follows:

> In many cases the Virgin blessed the crowds by movements of her hands. Following the apparition there were squads of doves that kept revolving around the dome for a few minutes and disappeared into thin air. Thousands of people witnessed this superb phenomenon.

These and other eyewitness accounts attest to the extraordinary reality of the apparition. But more extraordinary still are the photographs. The first photographs, taken in the early morning hours of April 13 by a photographer from Cairo, are not clear enough to be definitive. However, later photos clearly show the luminous figure on the roof of the church exactly as the eyewitnesses have described it. (Some of these photos are published in D. Scott Rogo's, *Miracles: A Parascientific Inquiry into Wondrous Phenomena.*)

The figure continued to appear frequently throughout April and May of 1968 and then somewhat less frequently during the rest of the year. In 1969, the full figure appeared only eleven times—although the "doves" and other phenomena sometimes appeared without the figure. The apparitions became even fewer in 1970 before finally stopping altogether in 1971.

This gradually decreasing pattern has led parascientific researcher D. Scott Rogo to suggest that the figure may have been the manifestation of a "thought form" created originally by the beliefs and expectations of the people who had visited St. Mary's Church during almost half a century, and then further energized by the thoughts of the hundreds of thousands of pilgrims who came to see it in 1968 and 1969. An interesting theory, to be sure, but it doesn't seem to explain the three-dimensionality and movement of the figure around the roof of the church. Nor does it explain how so many different people of different backgrounds and beliefs saw the same thing at the same time.

Whatever the cause of the manifestations, there is no question that the luminous figure of Zeitoun is one of the clearest and most striking proofs we have of a reality beyond the physical world.

I JUST FOUND GOD

DAVID PIERCE WAS RAISED IN LOS ANGELES BY PAR-
ents who were atheists. They taught him that the universe
is simply a huge machine, and that human beings are simply the product of biological and social forces. The idea
that there might be a "higher power" in the universe or a
deeper meaning to human life was simply not discussed.

Yet from an early age, it seemed that David was destined
for a different understanding. As a small child, he often
cried himself to sleep, feeling alone in the great big world
as children often do. One night through his tears he saw a
mysterious woman standing on his bed. She had long,
golden-red hair and wore a flowing, pale green gown with
a darker green pattern of diamonds. At each point where
the diamonds touched, an emerald pool of energy sparkled
like a magic gem. Since his parents never talked about angels, David concluded that the woman must be from outer
space. But wherever she came from, when she sat down
and held him in her arms, he felt a deep, warm unconditional love that guided him into pleasant sleep.

Despite this experience, David Pierce entered adulthood
a confirmed atheist, following the beliefs of his parents.
Tired of city life, he went away to a junior college nestled
in the foothills of the Sierra Nevada. There he drifted
through his academic classes, saving his real passion for
singing in choirs and other vocal groups—including one at
a local church, not because he had any interest in religion,
but just because he loved to sing.

During his second year at college, in April 1975, the
school vocal groups put on a big Saturday afternoon concert. As the performers arrived for the show, one of the
choir directors, a man named Ken, lashed out at everyone
and everything. He got into a shouting match with a key-
board player, and when the audience began to arrive, the
two men continued their argument behind the closed door
of the director's office. A few moments later, the startled
singers watched Ken toss the musician out of the office and
stalk off into the parking lot, where he drove off in his
Volkswagen Bug.

As the saying goes, the show must go on, and so it did—
with another director substituting for Ken. It wasn't exactly
a first-rate performance; in fact, after weeks of rehearsing
complex, difficult material, the concert was a major disappointment. For David, though, the real issue was Ken.
David respected and cared about Ken, not only as a musician and teacher, but as a friend. The preconcert behavior
was totally bizarre, totally unlike him. What was going on?
Had he flipped? Was he okay? What could David do to
help?

The following Monday, Ken was still missing, and David
found himself thinking about him instead of paying attention in class. Suddenly a voice spoke in his own mind: "Go
find Bob Pettit. You will find him here." As if in a day-
dream, a view of the college library was softly projected
on the chalkboard and David could clearly see Bob Pettit—
another member of the choir—sitting in a chair tipped back
against a bookcase, with his boots up on a table.

"When you have found him, take him here," the voice
continued. Now a different scene was projected on the
board—two sugar pines beside the campus pond, with the
shadow of one tree falling across the other tree.

The vision disappeared as the class ended, and David was
brought back to the daily world of slamming books and
scraping chairs. He didn't know what to think of the visions
on the chalkboard; they seemed so strange, so out-of-step
with all he believed. But he soon found himself outside the
school library, looking in from the same perspective he had

seen in the vision. Sure enough, there was Bob Pettit, lean-
ing back against the bookcase, with his booted feet up on
the table.

David went inside and told Bob that he was thinking
about going over to the pond and praying for Ken. Bob
said he'd been thinking about doing the same thing. For
David it was a very strange idea—an atheist going to pray.
But for Bob it seemed like the most natural idea in the
world. He was a Christian who wore his beliefs with a quiet
dignity, never trying to convince others to feel the same
way he did.

David didn't tell Bob about the visions, but he led him
to the exact spot he had seen, between the sugar pines. As
they settled cross-legged onto the ground, David noticed
that the shadow of the pine on their left was starting to
cross the pine on their right—just as he had seen in the
vision. Bob began to pray, and David found himself
strangely open to the words and the feelings of the prayer,
not resisting them with his usual cynicism.

When Bob finished, David closed his eyes and began to
say a prayer of his own. He didn't even know what he was
saying really; the words just came from within, flowing
outward as easily as Bob's words had flowed inward. Suddenly, a new vision appeared, far more powerful than the
ghostly outlines on the blackboard.

"As I spoke I saw a golden ring of light," David remembers today, "tilted and spinning like a disk in an infinite, pitch black void. Set upon the ring—like carousel
horses—were things that represented Ken's life as I knew
it. I saw the college, Ken's home, his family, a trumpet,
and other items spin past as the shining ring turned. I became subtly aware of a humming sensation between my
shoulder blades at the level of my heart."

David noticed that the one thing missing from the ring
was Ken himself. Still in the reverie, he spoke of finding
Ken and returning him to the wheel of his life. Suddenly a
rainbow emerged from the darkness, rising through the center of the golden ring and arching over the left horizon.
Now the humming became stronger, spreading up and

down his spine. Then slowly the end of the rainbow returned, carrying Ken and settling him softly onto the spinning golden ring.

As David watched the wheel of Ken's life, the warm humming filled his entire body until he felt as if he were floating above the ground. He opened his eyes to see if he really was floating, but he was still in contact with the earth—although his feelings told him otherwise. Then he gazed out across the pond. "Nothing had changed and yet it was all very different. Everything stood out vibrant and fresh. Then the awareness dawned: I was looking at absolute perfection! . . . The trees, the bushes, the people, the rocks, the earth, everything was so alive and seemed to be lit from within by a golden-red glow."

Now David focused on the sugar pine to his right, the one that the shadow had touched. It was glowing, and he could see every fine three-dimensional line of its delicate bark. He could even see a trail of dark ants climbing up the bark. It was so perfect that he wanted to touch it. When he rose to his feet, he found that every step brought a massive surge of energy, as if the entire earth was alive. And so it was. And so it is.

David continued to walk toward the tree, delighting in the blissful power that rose from the earth, shaking his soul with every step. He threw his head back and laughed with joy. It became a cosmic game. Could he actually reach the tree? Yes, he could. He caressed the fine-lined bark and marveled at the industrious ants. *Yep,* he thought, *perfect tree with perfect ants. Now what?* Now it was time to get on with his life.

Gradually the vision and jolts of energy faded. David and Bob left the pond, and made their way back to the everyday world—Bob to the library, David to the bus stop, where a female student smiled at the blissful expression on his face.

"Well, you certainly seem happy today," she said.

"I just found God," David replied—a strange statement to a stranger, but the young woman didn't even blink.

"I know," she replied. "You're glowing."

The following day, Ken, the missing choir director, returned to the college, saying only that he'd driven to Big Sur, where he sat and watched the whales go by. Maybe. And maybe Ken didn't need David's prayers at all. Maybe the one who really needed the prayers was David. For by the act of praying, the act of believing that there was a higher power and a deeper meaning, David Pierce's life changed forever.

"That day I awakened from the dream that the universe is only a huge machine," David says. "The Universe is alive! It is conscious and it is aware. I am not a hapless puppet. . . . I choose, therefore I am."

Today, David Pierce lives a life dedicated to spiritual growth and understanding. He travels around the country teaching people to make drums in a special way—with full awareness of where the materials come from, as a path to understanding our connection with the living earth. David's drum-making came out of another, more recent vision. But the turning point in his life was the day beside the college pond, the day he saw the golden disk and the arching rainbow, the day he felt the jolting power of the earth—the day he decided to pray for Ken.

Out of Body

During the early 1970s, psychic researchers Karlis Osis and Erlendur Haraldsson made two trips to India to investigate reports of extraordinary powers exhibited by Indian gurus. The story of Sai Baba's materializations is told in "Out of the Air" in February.

M ANY OF US HAVE HAD THE EXPERIENCE OF BEING SO busy that we wished we could "clone ourselves" and be in two places at once. As amazing as it may seem, the evidence is quite strong that some people can actually achieve this through conscious effort and for specific purposes. Many Christian mystics have been credited with the ability to project some form of their being to a distant place, often for the purpose of healing or preaching. And in India, where the relationship between guru and devotee has a very special spiritual meaning, gurus apparently use this power to stay in touch with their followers when they can't be with them in person.

During their visits to India, Karlis Osis and Erlendur Haraldsson investigated reports of bilocation by Indian gurus. They used two interesting criteria to narrow their field of research: the experience had to be witnessed by more than one person and the second, or astral, body had to be seen actually handling objects, thus establishing its reality in the physical world. Osis and Haraldsson followed up two intriguing stories and reported their findings in a paper at the

1975 convention of the Parapsychological Association.

One of the cases that the researchers tracked down involved Sai Baba, the famous holy man who had seemed to toy with them by materializing and dematerializing objects during their discussions about testing his powers under laboratory conditions. According to this story, while Sai Baba was visiting a palace on one side of the Indian peninsula, he appeared to Mr. Ram Mohan Rao, the director of a technical school on the other side of the peninsula. Mr. Rao then invited about twenty of his neighbors to a devotional service with the guru. Osis and Haraldsson were able to verify Sai Baba's physical presence in the palace, and they interviewed eight of the people who claimed to see him at the service.

This incident had occurred ten years earlier, time enough to allow inconsistencies to develop in the stories. However, the researchers found "reasonable agreement on the main points: a sadhu who looked like Sai Baba (whom they had seen only in pictures) was present in the school director's house for over an hour, sang some Sai Baba songs with them, produced holy ash in the way characteristic of Sai Baba, handled objects, and gave presents which the hosts still have."

Two other witnesses who had died since the incident apparently had not believed the visitor was really Sai Baba. These doubts, along with the time elapsed since the event, the inconsistencies in the stories, and the fact that the witnesses had never seen Sai Baba in person before the service, make this story intriguing but not fully convincing—although that doesn't mean it didn't happen. However, Osis and Haraldsson also investigated a stronger case of bilocation attributed to another Indian guru named Dadaji. Unlike Sai Baba, Dadaji led a worldly life as a singer and businessman before turning to the spiritual path. It's said that he received his training at an ashram in the Himalayas, where he took the name Dadaji, which means "elder brother."

In early 1970, Dadaji was visiting Allahabad, a city in north-central India. While staying with a group of his followers, he spent some time alone in a prayer room, and it is during this time of private meditation that the bilocation occurred. When he emerged from the room, he asked one of the women waiting outside to contact her sister-in-law in Calcutta and find out if he had been seen at a particular address in that city. The woman did as he asked, and the sister-in-law discovered a family named Mukherjee living at the address, who did indeed claim that they had seen Dadaji at that time. Calcutta is located in eastern India, about five hundred miles from Allahabad.

Because this incident occurred only a few years before their own visit, Osis and Haraldsson were able to interview everyone involved while memories were still fresh. The followers in Allahabad and the sister-in-law in Calcutta corroborated their parts of the story, but the most extraordinary revelations came from the Mukherjee family. All four members of the family—father, mother, son, and daughter—saw evidence of the apparition. The father was a banker and his son was a physician. Both of them had visited Dadaji on several occasions, but they were what might be called interested skeptics. Only the daughter, Roma, was a true believer who had visited the guru many times. The mother had never visited Dadaji.

The apparition began while Roma was lying on her bed, studying for an examination in English. According to Osis and Haraldsson, "She heard a noise and, on looking up, discovered Dadaji in the study which was visible to her through an open door. At first she could see objects in the room through him, and then he became solid. . . . Dadaji did not speak, but through sign language told her to be silent and to bring him a cup of tea. The door to the study was left slightly ajar while she went to the kitchen."

Roma screamed when she first saw Dadaji, which attracted the attention of her mother and brother. After she had poured the tea, they followed her back toward the study and watched Roma reach through the door to give Dadaji the tea and a biscuit. Her mother saw Dadaji through the crack in the door, but her brother, who was standing in a different position, only saw Roma hand the tea and the biscuit through the door and withdraw her hand without them. However, he agreed that there was nowhere inside the door where she could have set them down.

Around this time, the father returned from doing the morning shopping at the local bazaar. When his wife and children told him what had happened, he insisted on going to see for himself—even though they asked him to leave Dadaji alone. Peering though the crack in the door, he clearly observed the figure of a man sitting in the chair. The family then waited in their living room, where they could watch the door of the study.

"When they heard a noise and thought Dadaji had left," Osis and Haraldsson reported, "the family entered the study. The four of them saw that the door leading from the study to the stairwell was locked from the inside by an iron bar across it, and was also bolted from above. Dadaji was no longer there; half of the cup of tea and part of the biscuit were gone, and on the table was a cigarette, still burning— Dadaji's favorite brand!"

As a westerner raised in the years after the Surgeon General's Report, I can't help commenting that a being as evolved as Dadaji should know better than to smoke. But that may be a cultural difference. However, bilocation is not a cultural phenomena at all. For western stories of bilocation, see "The Flying Nun" in May and "A Power Divine" in June.

LOCKED GATE,
OPEN HEART

Here's another story of a young man's search for God during the confusing days of the early 1970s. But though the young man in this story is similar to David Pierce, the way that God chose to reveal Himself is intriguingly different.

BOB WAS ALMOST TWENTY-ONE YEARS OLD—FOOT-loose, free and open to just about anything the world had to offer. He had taken a break from his college classes back in the States and joined his family at a U.S. naval air station in southern Spain. In the classic style of his generation, Bob planned to spend the summer hitchhiking through Europe, and he decided to make a trial run to the tourist town of Torremolinos on the famous Costa del Sol. It was April 1973.

His last ride into the Torremolinos area came from an American minister. Bob liked him right away, and when the minister offered a place to spend the night, he accepted. Bob had never really been attracted to the minister's evangelical brand of Christianity, but he wasn't against it, either. The truth is that at that particular time and place, Bob was a young man searching for direction. "I was open," he remembers, "and the price was right."

The next morning, the minister drove him to a mission

on the outside of town, where travelers were allowed to stay—two days with no strings attached, as long as they wanted if they agreed to join the Christian activities of the house. A young American couple ran the mission, and Bob liked them too, especially the husband. His name was Tom, and though not an ordained minister, he was smart and articulate.

That afternoon Bob finally made it into Torremolinos, and there he met his temptation. Standing on a switchback high above the beach area, he caught a glimpse of long blonde hair that seemed to promise extraordinary beauty. Descending quickly, he wandered through the crowded streets hoping to find the girl connected to the hair, until he literally bumped into her in a gift shop. She was even more beautiful than he imagined, an American high school senior on a school trip to Spain. To Bob's amazement, this absolutely stunning girl was interested in him, and they spent the afternoon wandering along the beach. Today, Bob doesn't even remember the girl's name, but he recalls the miraculous events of the week with perfect clarity.

The next morning, Bob and Tom talked for hours, discussing questions of faith. When Bob admitted that he'd always had a tough time with Christian theology, Tom seemed to understand. In fact, the mission director seemed to be wrestling with his own faith, which only made his evangelism more compelling and intriguing. Finally, Tom left to join his afternoon prayer group and Bob was alone. With the intensity of a young man on a spiritual quest, he knew that he needed to make a very important decision.

"So I stood up," Bob remembers today, "closed my eyes and had a talk with God. I pointed out that I had four or five months free, and I was open. There was no reason why I couldn't spend the whole time here in the mission. I asked for guidance, for a sign. I cleared my mind of all the words, all the theology, and said, 'I'm here. If you want me for a Christian, take me.' I stood quietly for a few minutes . . . cracked my eyes to check for lightning. When it didn't come, I headed back to town."

That night Bob met the beautiful girl again, at a bar that

was popular with American tourists. She was happy to see him, and she was *so* sorry he wasn't staying in town. Bob was sorry, too. The mission had a "lights out" rule at 10:00, and he was supposed to be back by 9:45 if he wanted to spend the night. Amazingly enough, Bob managed to tear himself away from the girl and her friends a little after 9:30. He ran all the way up the hill, back to the mission, only to find a set of locked wrought-iron gates. Bob stared at the gates for a moment, turned on his heels, and ran back down to the bar, arriving just in time to catch the girl and her roommate heading to their hotel.

The girls managed to sneak the mission renegade past the front desk clerk and into their room, where Bob and the beautiful blonde squeezed into one narrow single bed. Just as they were settling in for the night, there was a loud pounding at the door, and the already wild evening turned even wilder. Bob spent the next two hours hiding in bathrooms and closets, running up and down staircases and dashing through long dark hallways, trying to avoid the clutches of the Guardia Civil—the paramilitary police force that had appointed themselves defenders of the American girls' virtue. It was like a David Niven movie mixed with the Marx Brothers and a touch of James Bond. In short, it was exactly the kind of adventure he was looking for.

Finally Bob managed to slip quietly back into the girls' room. "In a movie," he writes today, "the night would be one of unbridled passion." But this was reality, not a movie, and the passion was definitely missing. The next morning, Bob made his way back to the mission, where he faced Tom's anger and retrieved his few belongings. Tom had never locked the outside gate before, but he was deeply disappointed in the young American after their long conversation about faith.

Bob had asked for a sign and he'd received one: a locked gate, a gate that had never been locked before. He knew that he belonged in the town—not the mission—and that more adventure was waiting. But what adventure? What was the point of it all? He was still looking for something. And he was still open.

The next day, after the American high school girl left for home, Bob met another young woman on vacation. Her name was Annalei, and she was from Sweden. She didn't have the flashy surface beauty of the American blonde, but she had a deeper beauty, a beauty that resonated with Bob's heart and spirit. Their whirlwind courtship played out like a classier, more meaningful echo of the wild craziness he had experienced with the other girl. For the first time in a long while, Bob felt that his open heart might be answered with love.

Then, a few days after they met, Annalei developed a cold and bought an over-the-counter medication. That evening, the young couple were drinking wine in Annalei's hotel room with her roommate and a couple of German tourists. Annalei had only one full glass of wine, and she had just begun to sip her second glass when something went terribly wrong. Her eyes closed, her breathing slowed, and she slipped into unconsciousness. Then her breathing stopped. She was clearly dying.

Back in the States, Bob had worked as a lifeguard, and he started mouth-to-mouth resuscitation immediately. He still remembers how his deep emotional involvement with the lovely Swedish girl shifted into a strange clinical detachment. "I was falling madly in love with her," he says, "but as she went down I felt my emotions shut down with her, and the rest of the world was cut off. I was just breathing into a mouth to make a chest rise."

As he helped the dying girl, Bob could vaguely hear Annalei's roommate calling the hotel desk, desperately trying to explain that they needed a doctor immediately—not tomorrow, not in an hour—right now. He doesn't know how long he kept Annalei alive, at least ten minutes, maybe a half hour. Finally the hotel manager arrived with a doctor. At first, the doctor just watched Bob continue mouth-to-mouth; then he injected Annalei with a stimulant called atropine. Within moments, Bob could feel a change. Soon she was fighting his efforts, trying to breathe on her own, and as the life flowed back into her body, he felt his own emotions rushing back as well. She was no longer a malfunctioning physical machine stretched out on the bed. She was Annalei, the woman he was madly in love with. And he had saved her life.

In a movie, Bob and Annalei would have gotten married and lived happily ever after, raising a whole brood of beautiful Swedish-American children. But it didn't work out that way. Understandably disturbed by what had happened, Annalei left two days later and returned to Sweden. That summer Bob hitchhiked through Europe to visit her, but the magic they felt in Torremolinos had been lost. He couldn't quite tell what was wrong. Perhaps she had a boyfriend; perhaps she was still traumatized over her strange brush with death. Perhaps it was all just part of the plan.

Today, Bob believes that there were several messages in the locked gate at the mission. The most obvious, of course, was that he needed to be there to save Annalei. But the more subtle messages were for Bob himself, offering direction in his spiritual quest. It wasn't the right time for him to turn away from the world; he was young and he needed to experience life in all its myriad wonders. Moreover, Bob believes that the evangelical Christianity of Tom and the other people at the mission was not right for him. Years later, he found a more appropriate path for his own spirit in the very different Christianity of the Quakers.

My own interpretation of his experience is simply this: Each of us must ask our own questions of God, and if we ask with an open heart, we will receive the answer that is right for us. God knows what we need.

MAY

*For he has charged his angels
to guard you wherever you go . . .*

—PSALM 91

AN ANGEL
NAMED REBECCA

JANINE LAY IN HER BED, DESPERATELY TRYING TO FIND rest and comfort. It was May 1991. Just three days earlier, she had given birth to her third child, a beautiful daughter. Although the baby was healthy, the birth had been difficult and Janine had lost a great deal of blood. Now she was back at home, totally exhausted from the ordeal—so exhausted that sleep came fitfully when it came at all.

Suddenly, in the middle of the night, Janine woke to see a tall, bright light at the foot of the bed. In a flash, the light moved to her side, and she could clearly see a pair of hands reaching toward her. As the hands rested on Janine's shoulders, her whole body shook. Then the light disappeared, and Janine fell back into a deep, restful sleep—the best night's sleep she had experienced since the birth of her daughter.

Disturbed by this experience, Janine would only sleep with a night-light on for weeks afterward. But the experience was so powerful, so real, and so strange that she was determined to try and understand it. She went to the library and did extensive research, trying to find an explanation. But though she read for weeks, she found nothing. She was about to give up her search when one day she got a call from the librarian, saying they had another book for her. Janine said that she hadn't ordered any books, and she wasn't interested. She was tired of the search. But the librarian insisted that she come and get the book, saying, "I know that this is the book you want."

So Janine went to the library and picked up the book she hadn't ordered. It turned out to be *A Book of Angels* by Sophie Burnham, and in its pages, Janine found a story very similar to her own. For the first time, she realized that she had been touched by an angel. The discovery seemed even more amazing when she returned the book to the library, and the librarian admitted that she had no idea where it had come from.

Although Janine had never thought much about angels before, she decided to attend a workshop on angels at a local bookstore. During the workshop, the participants were directed to meditate in an attempt to contact their angels. The only meditation that Janine had ever done was during childbirth, but she tried to concentrate on her angel, asking the question, "What is my angel's name?"

"At that moment," Janine remembers, "the name Rebecca came 'screaming' through my mind. I refer to my angel as Rebecca now."

The woman conducting the workshop claimed to be psychic, and she told Janine that she was about to start on a journey and that everything would be okay. Janine wasn't a big believer in psychics, but the prediction combined with the "voice" of her angel convinced her that something unusual was about to happen. Two weeks later, it did.

All her life, Janine had suffered from pains in her chest. As a child, doctors had told her they were growing pains. When she stopped growing and they didn't go away, the doctors said it was all in her head. Janine tried to live with the pain, but it began to get worse, and her left arm hurt all the time. She had once had some lung problems, so she decided to go to a lung specialist. After a series of pulmonary tests, the doctor informed her that her lungs were in great shape. When she asked him what else could be wrong, he said that the only other available tests were cardiac, but that she was too young to be having heart problems. Janine was in her early thirties at the time. Once again, the doctor suggested that the pain was all in her head.

In the past, Janine had meekly accepted the "all in your head" diagnosis. But this time she blew up with a fury that was very unusual for her. She demanded that the doctor run a full battery of cardiac tests. Although he argued that they were just a waste of money, she demanded that he run them anyway.

The very next day, Janine received a call from her best friend, Patty, who asked what tests were being run. When Janine told her, Patty asked why they were not doing an echocardiogram. Janine had never heard of the test, and she didn't know anything about it—or why they weren't doing it. Patty was adamant that Janine have the echocardiogram.

With her new-found assertiveness, Janine called her doctor and demanded to have the test. He resisted, but she wouldn't take no for an answer. The other cardiac tests were inconclusive. But the final test—the echocardiogram—showed a hole in Janine's heart. Further testing indicated that the hole was about the size of a nickel. Surgery was scheduled for November 1993.

"I was lost in emotion, anxiety and fear," Janine remembers. "I just seemed to exist during those difficult days before my surgery." Two days before the surgery, Janine received a call from her friend Patty. When Janine admitted that she didn't know how she was going to find the courage to face the upcoming ordeal, Patty told her about two extraordinary dreams.

In the first dream, Patty stood on the edge of a canyon and called out Janine's name, the sound echoing and echoing within the canyon walls. An intuitive woman who had some personal experience with cardiac tests, Patty interpreted this dream as meaning that Janine should have an echocardiogram—and of course she was right.

The second dream had occurred just the night before. Janine's angel, Rebecca, had appeared to Patty and told her to deliver a new message to Janine—to tell her that everything was going to be all right. Janine was in such pain, Rebecca said, that she was unable to hear the angel herself. So Patty would have to deliver the message.

The message from Rebecca gave Janine new strength and courage to face the surgery. She put her affairs in order and entered the hospital. The surgery was extremely difficult. The surgeons cut across her chest horizontally, destroying most of the chest muscles. Then, once under the skin, they cut vertically, exposing the heart. The hole was much larger than expected—the size of a silver dollar.

After such extensive surgery, Janine faced a long, difficult recovery. She was in severe pain for weeks and couldn't sleep. Then one night, her angel Rebecca came to her again. This time, Janine couldn't see the angel, but she could feel her presence. She knew that Rebecca wanted her to roll onto her side, which was very difficult for Janine to do. But she did it anyway and felt Rebecca touch her back, sending vibrations throughout her body. The she fell into a sleep as deep and restful as the one the angel had inspired earlier.

Today, Janine has recovered, and she works as a volunteer at the same hospital where she had her surgery, helping other heart patients with their recovery. "I don't look at another thing the same," she says. "The dew on the trees makes me rejoice. A warm summer night brings me comfort. My children and family are precious. I feel like I glow inside from being so lucky. Every aspect of my life has changed."

And it all began with an angel named Rebecca.

THE FLYING NUN

Maria Coronel de Agreda was born to a Spanish middle-class family in 1602. When she was fifteen years old, for reasons that remain unclear, her entire family entered the religious life, separating along lines of gender. While her father and two brothers joined a Franciscan community in another town, Maria, her younger sister, and their mother converted their family house into a convent, where they were later joined by several other nuns.

From an early age, Maria exhibited a variety of mystical traits. She had visions, prayed intently, fasted often, and supposedly slept only two hours a night. Around the age of eighteen, she began to go into trances—or "ecstasies" in the terms of Catholic inspirational literature. According to a seventeenth century biographer, Maria resisted these trances so fiercely that she vomited blood. But nonetheless, they continued, growing deeper and deeper.

It is said that Maria levitated during her trances, but the reports are intriguingly understated. No one ever said she flew through the air; in fact, eyewitnesses claim she did not visibly rise from the ground at all. She simply hovered in a sort of weightless state, and the playful sisters discovered they could move her by blowing on her entranced body as if she were a feather. The other nuns were so impressed by this phenomenon that—while Maria remained insensible—they gently moved her closer to the outside walls of the convent, so that townspeople could blow through an opening in the grillwork and see the wonder for themselves.

(The walls and the grill were intended to protect the cloistered nuns from the influences of the outside world, but as Jesuit writer Herbert Thurston pointed out, "the convent was newly-founded, the community as yet very small, and the building ill-adapted for its religious purpose.")

This went on for some time, until Maria found out about it from a beggar who came to the gate of the convent. According to contemporary sources, she was so overcome with shame and humiliation that she loudly berated her fellow sisters and prayed to God that these miraculous manifestations would cease. Apparently they did, and there are no more reports of levitation or levity. Two nuns from a stricter convent in Madrid were transferred to Agreda, and a few years later, in 1627, Maria was elected Abbess. One of the first things she did was to begin building a new convent where she could levitate in peace, if she ever happened to levitate.

The levitations of Maria Coronel de Agreda seem strangely believable, because they are so simple. But Maria is also credited with another kind of "flying," what we would call astral projection or bilocation. And if the reports are true, the Spanish nun was one of the great astral flyers of all time.

It's unclear exactly when Maria's astral projections began, but it was probably sometime around 1620, the same year she began experiencing trances and levitation. According to her biographer, she experienced some five hundred of these spirit flights and in most of them she traveled to the New World, where Spanish priests were actively trying to convert the Indians. Maria reported many experiences during which she taught Christianity to a particular group of Indians. When they requested baptism, she told the group about some Franciscan missionaries who were working among other Indians, and gave them detailed instructions on how to get there.

At first Maria believed these experiences to be hallucinations, but after coming out of one trance she recalled distributing rosaries among the native people. She then discovered that the supply of rosaries in her cell had been depleted. Maria also recalled "seeing" the curvature of the earth at a time when some Europeans still believed the world to be flat.

The most persuasive proof of Maria's experiences came in 1630, when a Franciscan priest named Alonzo de Benavides returned to Spain from the New World. Father Benavides was in charge of the missions in the province of New Mexico, and he told his superiors that a group of Indians had come to him from afar, requesting baptism and saying a strange woman had appeared to them and taught them the Gospel. When he had shown the Indians a picture of a Franciscan nun wearing the same habit that Maria wore, the native people had immediately identified her as the mysterious woman.

Father Benavides met with Maria in Agreda and became convinced that she was indeed the woman who had appeared to the Indians. The cloistered nun—whose physical body apparently never left the Spanish convent—provided detailed descriptions of the Indians and of regions in Mexico that Benavides himself had seen. The priest included the story in an official report only four years later, which gives the strange experience a compelling stamp of authenticity.

In the material world, Maria Coronel de Agreda became one of the most powerful women in Spain, acting as a spiritual advisor to the troubled Emperor Philip IV. Maria and Philip exchanged over six hundred letters, with a startling level of honesty and respect on both sides of the correspondence. Today, however, Maria is even better known as the author of a mammoth work called *The Mystical City of God,* written after her reported flights to the New World. Maria claimed that this book came directly from God, declaring, "He willed me to write the whole work, without opinions, with nothing but the truth which the divine light would teach me." Today, *The Mystical City of God* is still considered among the classics of Christian mystical literature.

Did Maria Coronel de Agreda actually fly—astrally or otherwise—from her cell in a cloistered Spanish convent to an Indian tribe in the New World? Did she really distribute rosaries and direct the Indians to seek baptism among a group of Franciscan missionaries? We will never know for certain. But the life of the Spanish nun is undeniably intriguing. I picture her rising out of her cloistered cell, flying over the wide, wavy Atlantic, noticing the curvature of the earth, and landing in a new world, among mysterious men and women who hungered for knowledge of other cultures and beliefs. I like to think of Maria Coronel de Agreda as the original flying nun.

THE WOMAN IN THE ROSE DRESS

ESTELLE FIRST MET GRACE IN 1972, AT THE MAILBOXES in their apartment building in Evanston, Illinois. They discovered that they both subscribed to *Unity* magazine, an inspirational religious publication, and that connection led to a long and delightful friendship. Actually, it was a friendship of "couples," for Estelle and her husband often socialized and played bridge with Grace and her daughter Verne.

Grace was in her mid-seventies when they met, and Estelle was impressed by her well-groomed beauty; she always looked just perfect. For Verne, however, perfection was a constant struggle. She suffered from cerebral palsy, but she did all she could to live a normal life—not only for herself, but also to please her "perfect" mother. She took public transportation every day to work for a group of lawyers in downtown Chicago. And when Estelle and her husband joined them for bridge, Verne insisted on setting up the table and chairs herself, striving to be the perfect hostess regardless of her disability.

The years passed. Estelle and her husband moved to a house in the nearby suburb of Skokie, while Grace and Verne moved to another apartment in Evanston near Calvary Cemetery, a beautiful old cemetery that opens up onto a sweeping vista of Lake Michigan. Later Estelle and her husband returned to Evanston, while Grace and Verne moved to Tennessee, where another daughter lived. Estelle stayed in touch, and the two pairs of friends traveled back and forth several times to visit.

The last time that Estelle saw Grace was in Tennessee, during May 1985. She was in her late eighties and her health was poor, yet she looked as lovely as ever. One evening, the old bridge foursome went out to dinner and a play at an outdoor theater. They arrived early for the play, so they just sat in the woodsy setting, enjoying each other's company in the warm spring evening. Estelle marveled at how beautiful and full of life Grace was, despite her poor health. She wore a rose-colored dress with black patent leather pumps, and her white hair was curled and waved to perfection.

A month later, Grace's condition had deteriorated, particularly her circulatory system, and her doctor said that only amputation of her foot might prolong her life. It was a difficult decision, and her daughters weighed it carefully. Finally they decided that, considering their mother's advanced age and the pride she had always taken in her appearance, it would be best to let nature take its course. Grace died shortly afterward, on July 18, 1985.

When Estelle heard of Grace's death, she was deeply sorry to lose a good friend. But her greatest concern was for Verne, who had lived with her mother all her life. Estelle knew the loss would be extremely painful and difficult.

Fall became winter, and winter became spring. Once again, it was May. One morning, Estelle was riding the elevated train from Evanston to her teaching job in Chicago. Though she had a window seat, her nose was buried in a book. She'd made this journey countless times before and seen all there was to see. Or so she thought.

As the train rattled along above Calvary Cemetery, Estelle happened to look up from her book and gaze out the window. There was Grace, standing in a bed of daisies among the graves, smiling and laughing and waving at her. She wore the rose-colored dress and the black patent leather pumps, and her white hair was perfectly coifed. Above the noise of the train, Estelle could hear Grace's laughter clearly. She waved and smiled back, as if it were the most natural thing in the world. Then she realized what she was doing, and noticed the strange look from her fellow commuter in the seat bedside her. "Oh my God!" she muttered. And Grace disappeared.

Estelle contacted Verne in Tennessee and told her what she had seen. She believed that Grace was trying to tell them that she was happy and at peace, and that her daughters should have no second thoughts about the decision they had made in the last days of her life. For Verne, this message from her mother was a great source of strength in a difficult time, an affirmation of the eternal love and connection between mother and daughter though they could no longer be together on this earth.

Why did Grace appear to Estelle instead of Verne? Perhaps Verne was still in too much pain to open her heart and spirit. This is a common pattern in apparitions of those who have recently died. It seems that it's easier for people who are not so intensely involved with the loss to see the spirit of the one who has passed. Estelle missed Grace, too, of course, but her loss was not so personal and immediate. So she was able to see Grace dancing on the daisies in her rose-colored dress, and to deliver the message to Verne, who needed so desperately to hear it.

Shortly before she met Grace, Estelle had another miraculous experience that led to her marriage. For that story, see "Meeting Mr. Right" in June.

THE CROSS IN THE
BATHROOM WINDOW

AROUND THREE IN THE MORNING ON MAY 21, 1994, Maria Ortega was awakened from a sound sleep by the cry of a newborn child. At least that's what it sounded like initially, and it seemed to come from the bathroom of their house in Santa Ana, California. When Maria turned on the bathroom light, she heard a sound like the rush of the wind, and saw a brilliant cross of light in the bathroom window.

"I have never felt that frightened," Maria later told a reporter. "When I saw it, I got down on my knees and started to cry."

Maria told her family and friends about the cross, and the story spread like wildfire. Within days, the Ortegas were deluged with pilgrims eager to see the miracle in their bathroom window. Visitors came from all over southern California, and some even journeyed from northern California and Mexico. At the peak of excitement, the Ortegas faced between three hundred and seven hundred visitors every night.

Each of them saw the glowing cross whenever the bathroom light was turned on. It was no illusion, no foggy vision in the middle of the night. It was very real, and sometimes more than one cross appeared in the glass. A large cross with a smaller cross beneath it shows clearly in a newspaper photograph taken from outside the Ortegas' house in June.

The crush of visitors became so overwhelming that the owners of the house—from whom the Ortegas were renting—decided to remove the pane of glass and give it to the local Catholic church, Immaculate Heart of Mary, where it was displayed for all to see. The glass was set on an easel and illuminated, producing the same glowing cross that Maria Ortega had seen in her bathroom.

Some months later, the Ortega family moved out of the house, which now had a different pane of glass in the bathroom window. Feeling that the miracle furor had passed, the pastor of Immaculate Heart of Mary returned the original pane to the Ortega family, who took it with them to their new home.

The cross in the Ortegas' bathroom window is only one of many such apparitions that have been reported from all over the world. On August 27, 1971, a huge glowing cross appeared in a window of Chapel of Faith Baptist Church in downtown Los Angeles. The cross reappeared every day around the same time, in the late afternoon as the setting sun shone through the window. Although skeptics assumed that it was just a trick of the light, the pastor of the church pointed out that no one had ever seen it before in the six years they'd occupied the building.

The Los Angeles cross set off a series of similar apparitions throughout the fall of 1971, first in Florida, then in Georgia, and finally in New York City. To begin with, the crosses appeared only in churches, but they soon spread to private homes as well. These apparitions, called the Great Cross Flap of 1971, echoed a bizarre series of apparitions in Germany a century earlier. There the crosses appeared in the windows of private homes, first in the town of Baden-Baden and then in the neighboring town of Rastadt.

On a purely physical level, most of these crosses can probably be explained by some property of the glass refracting the light. But why do the crosses suddenly appear out of nowhere, in panes of glass where no one ever saw crosses before? And why do they spread from one window to another like a bizarre epidemic of light? Psychic researcher D. Scott Rogo suggests that, during the Great

Cross Flap of 1971, the mental energy of the various church congregations may have projected a "psychic field" around the windows that bent the light to form the cross. But that hardly explains the cross in the Ortegas' bathroom window; nor does it explain why Maria Ortega heard the cry of a newborn child or a sound like the rushing of the wind.

Perhaps the answer is that there is no answer, and we should simply accept these apparitions as small miracles that help us search for deeper meaning in this all-too-physical world. That's what Deacon John Shimotsu of the Immaculate Heart of Mary church felt when he saw the cross in the Ortegas' bathroom window. "It is something beautiful," he said. "People here are very spiritual, and if it makes them pray, then fine."

IF I HAVE ANY POWER LEFT

Sometimes a small miracle may be only the tip of the iceberg—a sign of a greater and more awesome power that has faded into the mists of time. So it is, I believe, in this account of an old Lakota holy man who made rain on a cloudless day.

IN MAY 1931, TWO EXTRAORDINARY MEN—HOST AND guest—worked together on the Pine Ridge Reservation of South Dakota. The host was Nicholas Black Elk, a Lakota holy man. The guest was John G. Neihardt, the poet laureate of Nebraska. Black Elk was sixty-three years old, a weary, wizened survivor of a half-century of cultural destruction at the hands of the *Wasichu*—the others. John Neihardt was 50, a man of letters at the height of his powers. He was *Wasichu*—one of the others, but different than those who had come before. And Black Elk knew it the moment he met him.

"As I sit here," Black Elk said, "I can feel in this man beside me a strong desire to know the things of the Other World. He has been sent to learn what I know, and I will teach him."

The heart of Black Elk's story was an extraordinary vision that came to him as a nine-year-old boy in 1873, before the *Wasichu* destroyed the culture of his people. After a fall from a horse, he lay unconscious in his family's tipi for twelve days while he was taken on a tour of the spirit world. Black Elk's vision is among the most detailed and powerful in the annals of spiritual literature, far too complex to discuss here. But to understand the small miracle of 1931, we must understand this:

Black Elk believed that he was entrusted with a great mission by the powers of his vision. He believed that it was his responsibility to save the Lakota nation—or to put it in his own terms, "to make the tree flower within the sacred hoop." And sadly, by the time Black Elk told his story to John Neihardt, he was convinced that he had completely failed in his mission. The hoop of the nation lay shattered, and the once-proud Lakota struggled to adapt to the ways of the *Wasichu*. Black Elk himself became a Catholic, he told Neihardt, "because my children have to live in the world."

In late May, when he had finished telling his story, Black Elk pointed to Harney Peak, looming on the horizon—the highest mountain in the sacred Badlands of South Dakota. "There, when I was young," he said, "the spirits took me in my vision to the center of the earth and showed me all the good things in the sacred hoop of the world. I wish I could stand up there in the flesh before I die, for there is something I want to say to the Six Grandfathers."

Black Elk and John Neihardt agreed to visit Harney Peak together. A few days later, they drove toward the Black Hills in a two-car caravan, with Black Elk and his son, Benjamin, in one car, and John Neihardt and his two daughters, Enid and Hilda, in the other. Benjamin had acted as translator throughout the sessions, while Enid acted as stenographer.

On the morning of May 30, the group left their tourist cabin at Sylvan Lake and hiked to the top of the mountain. Although Black Elk's spirit was eager, his body was tired and he had to stop often to rest. But on the way up, the old man said to his son, "Something should happen today. If I have any power left, the thunder beings of the west should hear me when I send a voice, and there should be at least a little thunder and a little rain.''

"It was a bright and cloudless day," John Neihardt later wrote, "and after we had reached the summit the sky was perfectly clear. It was the season of drouth [drought], one of the worst in the memory of the old men.''

When they reached the top, Black Elk stepped behind a rock, took off his *Wasichu* clothes, and put on long red underwear—apparently a substitute for the red body paint of his vision, though it may have been out of respect for Neihardt's daughters. Then he put on a dark breechcloth, high stockings, beaded moccasins, and a buffalo-hide headdress decorated with eagle feathers. In his left hand he held a sacred pipe with a single eagle tail feather symbolizing *Wakan Tanka*, the Great Mysterious. He held his right hand palm outward, stretched skyward in prayer.

He cried out four times, one for each of the four directions: "Hey-a-a-hey! Hey-a-a-hey! Hey-a-a-hey! Hey-a-a-hey!" Then he began to pray, a long beautiful prayer recorded by Enid Neihardt in her notebook. In essence it was a prayer to save his people. He recounted how the Six Grandfathers—the six powers of the earth—had set him on this spot and shown him all the good things, and he admitted his own failings in not carrying out his mission to make the tree bloom. "But there may be a root that is still alive," he prayed, "and give this root strength and moisture of your good things. . . .''

As he neared the end of his prayer, the old man's voice rose to a singing wail. "In sorrow I am sending a voice, O six powers of the earth, hear me in sorrow. With tears I am sending a voice. May you behold and hear me that my people will live again.''

Suddenly, out of a clear blue sky, a few thin clouds gathered overhead and a fine cold rain began to fall, with low rumbles of thunder echoing across the Badlands. Black Elk stood silently, tears running down his cheeks, his face gazing up into the rain. The thunder beings had heard his voice, just as he had predicted, "if I have any power left." Then the sky cleared as quickly as it had clouded, and the heavens were perfectly blue again.

When they descended from the mountain, Black Elk and John Neihardt parted company. The experience of telling his story seemed to rejuvenate the old man, and for the rest of his life Black Elk worked to preserve the spiritual traditions of his people. He participated again in tribal dances and played the role of a Lakota medicine man in an annual tourist pageant in the Black Hills, performing sacred rituals in hopes that the *Wasichu* might see them and appreciate them. During the 1940s he collaborated on another book with John Neihardt, a history of the Lakota called *When the Tree Flowered,* and worked with anthropologist Joseph Epes Brown on an account of the seven Lakota religious rites called *The Sacred Pipe.* Black Elk died in 1950 at the age of eighty-six.

John Neihardt went home to Nebraska, where he wrote his book based on the lessons of the holy man. That book, *Black Elk Speaks,* had a curious, perhaps miraculous, history of its own. First published in 1932, it received glowing reviews but quickly died on the shelves of American bookstores. In the bleak days of the Depression, people had little money for books—and most whites had little interest in the old ways of the American Indian people. Yet somehow, a single copy made its way to Zurich, Switzerland, where it was admired by Carl Jung and other German scholars. Their interest in the book passed back across the Atlantic, and in 1961, almost thirty years after the original edition, the book was republished.

This time it found a large, eager following among a new generation of whites and Indians. For whites it was an eye-opening journey into another culture, another spiritual perspective, but for American Indians it was something more—a direct connection to their own spiritual roots. As Indian scholar Vine Deloria, Jr., wrote, "... the book has become a North American bible of all tribes."

Although some now feel the book contains too much of John Neihardt and not enough of Black Elk, there are many others who recognize the book for what it is: the answer in some small way to Black Elk's prayer on Harney Peak. For in the hearts and minds of those who have read it, *Black Elk Speaks* has made the tree bloom once again in the sacred hoop of the Lakota nation.

JUNE

Why, who makes much of a miracle?
As to me I know of nothing else but miracles . . .
To me every hour of the light and dark is a miracle,
Every cubic inch of space is a miracle.

—WALT WHITMAN, "MIRACLES"

THE FLYING FRIAR

There have been many stories of levitating saints, but the most amazing—and best authenticated—are the stories of Saint Joseph of Cupertino. Although Joseph lived in the seventeenth century, there were an impressive number of eyewitnesses and sworn documents attesting to his flights.

JOSEPH DESA WAS BORN ON JUNE 17, 1603, IN THE southern Italian village of Cupertino. As a young boy he demonstrated a simple-mindedness that characterized him throughout his life. He would forget to eat and wander around the village, dazed and slack-jawed as if he couldn't remember where he was supposed to be going. After failing as a shoemaker's apprentice, he tried to enter the religious life, only to be turned down by two different orders because of his clumsiness and apparent stupidity. Finally, through the influence of two uncles who were Franciscan friars, he was accepted as a lay servant at the nearby monastery of Grotella, where he was put to work in the stables.

Although Joseph never won any awards for high intelligence, he impressed the monks with his sweet good-nature, his humility, and his piety. Like many Christian mystics, he practiced severe austerities of the flesh—long periods of fasting and prayer, self-flagellation and wearing a "hair shirt." In 1625, the Franciscans accepted him into the religious order and he began to study for the priesthood.

Three years later he was ordained, although he could barely read and write and couldn't grasp the main points—let alone the fine points—of theology. In a preliminary examination, it's said that the bishop happened to turn at random to the only passage in the Gospels that Joseph had anything to say about. In the final examination, the first candidates did so well that the others—including Joseph—were not examined at all. If these stories are true, it seems that the hand of God had already touched Joseph of Cupertino. But it was only the beginning.

After his ordination in 1628, Joseph began to experience ecstatic trances in which he would emit a shrill cry and suddenly rise from the ground, often flying a substantial distance through the air. These ecstasies might be set off by anything that filled his spirit with the wonder of God: the words of the Mass, the sight of a religious statue, even an off-hand remark. When he returned to his senses, the simple friar would laugh in embarrassment and apologize for his "fits of giddiness."

According to one story, Joseph was walking in the monastery garden with a visiting priest who happened to comment on the beauty of the heaven that God had created. With his shrill cry, Joseph took off and landed on the top of an olive tree, where he knelt in prayer, barely shaking the branch. Although Joseph usually returned to the ground during his levitations, in this particular case he came out of the trance while still in the tree and the other priest had to go and get a ladder to help him down.

According to an even wilder story, the monks were building a model of Calvary with three huge crosses. They had set the two smaller side crosses in place, but the middle cross, about thirty-six feet high, was so heavy that ten men had struggled without success to set it into the hole. Seeing their struggle, it's said that Joseph flew some seventy yards through the air, picked up the huge cross "as if it were a straw" and dropped it into place.

The flight to the top of the olive tree was reported by the fellow priest who witnessed it, but the story of the cross was not set down until at least thirty years after the actual event, so there's probably a good dose of exaggeration in the tale. But whether or not these particular stories are true in all their details, it seems clear that Joseph of Cupertino did indeed defy the laws of gravity on a fairly regular basis. There are more than one hundred written reports of levitations, including over seventy during the years he spent at the monastery in Grotella.

Perhaps the strongest evidence that some of these early reports must be true is the reaction of Joseph's superiors. As news of the "flying friar" spread through the countryside, the monastery was so besieged by curious visitors that Joseph was not allowed to say Mass in public, eat with his fellow monks, or make other public appearances—an extremely unusual restriction that remained in effect for thirty-five years, from shortly after his ordination in 1628 to his death in 1663. Obviously, something very strange was going on.

In 1638, after ten years of flying, Joseph was summoned to Naples where he was examined three times by the Inquisition, before finally being released. He was then taken to Rome, where he had an audience with Pope Urban VIII. At the sight of the "Vicar of Christ," Joseph immediately went into an ecstasy and took off into the air. Catholic pontiffs—even in the seventeenth century—have been rather reticent about miracles, but the pope was so impressed that he said if Joseph died before he did, he would testify to the miracle he had witnessed.

Despite Urban's response, the Catholic Church has always been a bit embarrassed by living mystics, and Joseph was transferred to a monastery in Assisi, the home of St. Francis himself. There, hundreds of miles from his boyhood village, the flying stopped for two years while Joseph suffered from a severe psycho-spiritual depression, feeling that God's grace had left him. Then the ecstasies began again— just as miraculously as before. Unlike Joseph's earlier levitations, some of these later flights were recorded shortly after their occurrence and reported by eyewitnesses of high social standing who had little to gain by spreading nonsense.

In 1645, Admiral Juan Alfonso Henriquez de Cabrera, the Spanish ambassador to the Papal Court, visited Joseph in his cell and was so impressed by his simple piety that he told his wife, "I have seen and spoken with another St. Francis." When his wife asked to meet this amazing person, the ambassador arranged to override the prohibition against public appearances, although Joseph warned him that he might not be able to speak to her. Sure enough, when Joseph entered the church for the meeting, his eyes focused on a statue of Mary and he immediately took off, flying over the heads of the ambassador, his wife, and their large group of followers. After hovering before the statue, he flew back over their heads and returned to his cell in embarrassment. This story was corroborated by many eyewitness depositions from the members of the ambassador's retinue.

Another well-attested story involves Johann Friedrich, Duke of Brunswick and Hanover. Although he was a Lutheran, the duke was so intrigued by reports of the flying friar that he traveled to Assisi and arranged for himself and two aides to secretly watch Joseph celebrating the Mass. On two successive days, the visitors observed the monk leave the ground in ecstasy, once hovering in the air for fifteen minutes. The duke was so impressed by what he saw that he converted to Catholicism—at a time when the distinction between Catholic and Protestant was far more politically charged than it is today.

Despite the attention of such noble visitors, the Church again became disturbed by the publicity over Joseph's levitations and the Inquisition ordered him sent to an isolated monastery run by a different religious order. But there too the wonders continued, bringing a new onslaught of curious pilgrims. So Joseph was transferred again, and yet again. He spent the last six years of his life at a monastery of his own order in Osimo, with only a few approved visitors from among his fellow monks. Yet even these few saw miracles: Joseph rising seven or eight feet to kiss a statue of the Infant Jesus and later flying with the statue in his cell; Joseph embracing a fellow friar in the midst of ecstasy and carrying him into the air.

After a short illness, Joseph died on September 18, 1663 at the age of sixty. Investigations into his life began soon afterward, and it is from this period that most of the written testimony can be dated. The eyewitness accounts of the monks at Osimo were set down—under oath—only four or five years after the events.

During canonization proceedings, the Church assigns an official to play the role of "devil's advocate," arguing against the evidence for sainthood. In Joseph's case, this role was assumed by Prosper Lambertini, the Church's greatest authority on the subject of miracles. A man with an impressive analytical mind, Lambertini used all his mental powers to criticize the alleged miracles of Joseph's life. But he apparently convinced himself of their truth in the process, for it was Lambertini himself—after he had become Pope Benedict XIV—who issued the decree of Beatification, the second of three steps on the road to Catholic sainthood. In this decree, Benedict wrote that "eyewitnesses of unchallengeable integrity gave evidence of the famous upliftings from the ground and prolonged flights of the aforesaid Servant of God when rapt in ecstasy." Joseph was canonized by the Catholic Church in 1767.

The story of Joseph of Cupertino is one of the strangest and strongest cases of levitation in the historical record. Here we have a simpleminded friar, with no political or economic power, who was considered a rather embarrassing nuisance for his entire priestly career. Yet, highly-respected and otherwise rational observers—including a pope, a duke, and an ambassador—reported that they had seen him fly through the air. And the Catholic Church, which does not take miracles or sainthood lightly, canonized him on the basis of these reports.

Of course the case would be stronger if we had his levitations on video tape or if they occurred in the 1940s rather than 1640s. But the fact that Joseph lived in the seventeenth century doesn't mean he didn't levitate. We believe other historical records from this time—for example, the Mayflower Compact or the diary of Massachusetts Governor John Winthrop. And we would have no problem believing a report by the Spanish ambassador or the Duke of Brunswick regarding the events of a war or the negotiation of a treaty. Why then, should we not believe their reports of a simpleminded friar who flew on the wings of faith?

God Will Do
All the Rest

In 1965, Virginia Shotwell left her home in Rochester, New York and walked toward her car, carrying a stack of some twenty books that needed to be returned to the library. As she crossed the blacktop driveway, she stepped onto an oil slick left by the car and slipped awkwardly toward the side, her right knee crashing hard onto her left leg and ankle.

Virginia's husband rushed her to the nearest emergency room, where the ER physician ordered a series of X rays. "We happen to have an excellent orthopedist in the hospital right now, visiting a patient," the physician told Mr. Shotwell. "Dr. Kalin. If it's all right with you, we'll just call him in, rather than contacting your own doctor."

Mr. Shotwell agreed, and Dr. Kalin arrived in the ER to examine the X rays. Like many orthopedic surgeons, Dr. Kalin had a reputation as a brilliant technician with a poor bedside manner. But he proved extremely sensitive in the case of Virginia Shotwell.

Virginia's left ankle was totally shattered, with loose bones scattered around the area, and the left leg was broken in two places. The damage was so extensive that Dr. Kalin decided not to show Virginia the X rays, discussing them only with her husband. He felt that there was no chance that she would ever walk again without a limp and little chance that she would walk without pain. He wanted to spare her the bad news until after the bones were set.

In unbearable pain, Virginia accepted a painkiller but demanded to stay conscious while the bones were set. Dr. Kalin requested that two interns be allowed to watch the procedure and Virginia gave permission. Just before he started, the doctor looked Virginia in the eye and said, "I promise you I will do the very best I can."

"You do that," she said, "and God will do all the rest."

Since she was awake during the procedure, Virginia could follow the whole discussion between the orthopedist and the interns. Years later, she described the complicated procedure as clearly as if it had been yesterday:

"He had to take the foot, lift it away from the socket, pull it down, bring it forward beyond my ankle, and then push it into the right place, at the same time he showed them that the leg bones had to be in a certain angle with the knee. One of them held my leg as the doctor—while keeping the foot in place—took his other hand and gathered the loose bones around the ankle area."

After the procedure, Dr. Kalin informed Virginia that she would have to stay in the hospital overnight, and that she was scheduled for surgery the next morning. Setting the bone was only the beginning. He would have to insert a pin into her ankle, but he wouldn't know where to position it until examining new X rays of the bones after setting.

The next morning, when the doctor entered Virginia's hospital room, his face was white as a sheet—as if he'd just seen a ghost. "No way is he going to operate on me today," Virginia thought. But of course she didn't say it. Instead she simply greeted him with a "How are you?"

"Apparently there's been some mistake," Dr. Kalin told her. "We'll have to take some additional X rays."

So Virginia went down to radiology for another set of X rays. But they only confirmed the previous set. There was no need for a pin. No need for surgery. Every bone was in place. And Virginia Shotwell recovered to walk without a limp, recovered to walk without pain.

The work of a fine orthopedist? Certainly. But it was the orthopedist who refused to believe the X rays of his own work. Perhaps it was God who took care of the rest.

MEETING MR. RIGHT

*In May, I told the story of Estelle's poignant vision of a
friend named Grace who had recently died. Fifteen years
earlier, just before she met Grace, Estelle had an equally
extraordinary experience that led to the love of her life.*

FOR TWENTY-FOUR YEARS, ESTELLE WAS TRAPPED IN AN
unhappy marriage to an abusive alcoholic. Finally, with the
help of a psychiatrist, she took charge of her life and ter-
minated the marriage. She knew it was the right thing to
do. Their children were almost grown, and Estelle felt free
to make a new life for herself. In her late forties, she was
an attractive, vibrant woman who hoped for a second
chance.

On June 5, 1971, about two years after the divorce, Estelle went with her sister and two other friends for a reading
with Mr. Psychic, famous from his appearances on television. Each woman wrote a question on a sheet of paper and
placed it in a sealed envelope, with only her initials on the
outside to identify it. Estelle's question was, "When will I
meet Mr. Right?"

Mr. Psychic took Estelle's unopened envelope and
placed it on his forehead, saying, "You have been through
a crucifixion and you are going to have a resurrection. You
have met this man, and in a month you will meet him again.
You will be very happy, and you will travel all over the
world."

Estelle smiled at the prediction. It sounded nice, but she hadn't met anyone lately, and she didn't place much stock in psychics anyway—although the fact that he had answered her question without opening the envelope was intriguing. As for the rest, well . . . time would tell.

A month later, on the Fourth of July, Estelle was invited by her sister's friend to come over and help teach her brother how to play bridge. The brother's name was John Stephan, and Estelle had met him briefly once before. But he certainly didn't seem like the man of her dreams. He was quite a bit older—sixty-five years old, while Estelle had just turned fifty. John was a pharmacist, and his wife had recently died. Estelle could read between the lines— obviously her sister and her friend were trying to "set them up," but Estelle wasn't all that interested.

Over the bridge table, John told Estelle about his experiences in World War II, and how it had felt when he first crossed the Atlantic. Suddenly an inner voice spoke in Estelle's mind, saying, *I'd like to travel with you.* She was shocked at the thought. Where had it come from? She immediately squashed the idea, saying to herself, *No I wouldn't. He's too old for me.*

Nonetheless, when John asked Estelle out on a date, she accepted and they began to date regularly. He took her to plays and fine restaurants, and she enjoyed being with him. But she didn't feel that special chemistry she was looking for. Finally, after three months Estelle told John that she didn't want to see him anymore, that their paths were different and she had to go her own way.

John was crushed. His feelings for Estelle had grown stronger every day. But he was gallant in accepting her rejection. "All right," he said. "I care deeply for you, but if that's what you want, well that's it."

Several months passed, and Estelle still hadn't met that special man she was looking for. Then suddenly, tragedy struck. Her twenty-three-year-old daughter grew critically ill with Hodgkin's disease, and the cancer spread like wildfire. Fortunately, the surgeons were able to remove all the cancerous cells, and her daughter gradually recovered. But it was a very difficult time.

During this period, Estelle met John again at a gathering of the Lamplighters, a singles group sponsored by the local Presbyterian church. He was very sympathetic about her daughter's illness, and he asked her out again. Feeling a need for a shoulder to lean on, she accepted and they began another period of dating. But this time, Estelle found herself seeing more and more of the good things about John Stephan.

After several months, John asked Estelle to marry him. She told him she wasn't ready, and he agreed to wait. A month later, she said, "Yes," but this time John surprised her by suggesting they wait a little longer. He wanted her to be sure. And perhaps he had second thoughts himself. John's own marriage of twenty-seven years had been almost as unhappy as Estelle's marriage. Naturally, they were both hesitant to try again.

Estelle turned to God for guidance. "I must have an answer," she prayed. "This indecision is driving me crazy!" As many Christians do in times of crisis, she opened her Bible looking for an answer. She gazed in amazement at the words on the top of the page—chapter 16, verse 17 of Paul's first letter to the Corinthians: "I am glad of the coming of Stephanos and Fortunatus and Achaicus; for that which was lacking on your part they have supplied."

I am glad of the coming of Stephanos . . . John's last name was Stephan. There was her answer.

Estelle called John immediately and told him what had happened. She said she would marry him, and that the wedding should be on June 17—for the 17th verse where she had found her answer.

"Fine honey," John replied. "I'm glad you're sure."

John and Estelle were married for over twenty years, a wonderful, blissful second chance. Despite his age, John proved to be young at heart, younger in many ways than Estelle. They shared friends and family, and treasured their love for each other. Every summer, they traveled all over the world, just as Mr. Psychic had predicted.

Was Mr. Psychic's prediction a miracle? Maybe. Was the message in the Bible a miracle? Probably. But for Estelle Stephan, the real miracle was John, the man who gave her a second chance at love.

"He was my miracle," she says today. "And to think that I was saying no to this wonderful gift."

A POWER DIVINE

The experiences of Ed Morrell inspired a book by Jack London called The Star Rover. *Later, Morrell wrote an autobiography,* The Twenty-Fifth Man, *in which he told the true story as he saw it. The following account is based on Morrell's book, with some of the more earthly details confirmed by objective sources.*

IN 1898, A PRISONER NAMED ED MORRELL WAS SENtenced to a life of solitary confinement in the bowels of San Quentin—only the second man in the history of the prison to receive such a harsh sentence. Morrell was a "lifer" to begin with, locked away for his activities with a gang of train robbers called the California Outlaws. But life among the general prison population was one thing; life in solitary was something else.

"My dungeon cell was four and a half feet wide by eight feet long," Morrell later wrote. "It allowed me but three short steps and a turn on the fourth as exercise. I had an old straw tick on the floor and two blankets. A scanty meal and water were shoved in through the bottom of the grated door once every twenty-four hours. . . . Silence and darkness completed the tragedy. I was alone, a grim life convict dead and forgotten in a living tomb."

By the time he was thrown into the solitary cell, Morrell had already survived a horrible succession of tortures—first at Folsom prison and then at San Quentin. In those days, torture was the dirty little secret of American prisons. Morrell was hung by his shackled wrists for hours at a time, day after day. He was locked in a special cell and gassed with chloride of lime. In another torture cell, he and seven other prisoners were held in cold water up to their necks. After these tortures Morrell recalled, "I was a changed man. The iron of hate had branded my heart."

But the physical tortures were overshadowed by the mental tortures of solitary. At first, Morrell played mental games to maintain his sanity. He tried to project his mind beyond the confines of the cell walls. He developed a new irrigation system and played mental checkers. He even tried to communicate with the flies in his cell, becoming convinced that they had distinct personalities just like human beings. But as the months dragged into years, he feared he would lose his mind. If only he could communicate with another human being.

The only other convict in the dark, solitary world was Jake Oppenheimer, locked up thirteen cells away. Morrell decided to convey a "knuckle code," by which they could communicate through rapping on the prison walls. Each day, when Morrell grew tired of rapping, he would visualize the code in his mind, hoping to communicate it through mental telepathy. Finally after nine months of effort, Jake rapped out the code in perfect order. As they continued to "talk," the other prisoner indicated that the code came to him "just like a flash—a vision—the picture of a square seemed photographed on the wall."

This was Ed Morrell's first proof that he could project his mind. But it was only the beginning. A new warden took over San Quentin, a brutal, one-eyed man who vowed to break the spirit of Ed Morrell once and for all. Morrell had been sentenced to solitary for his part in a failed prison rebellion. A stool pigeon claimed that only Morrell knew where they had hidden a cache of smuggled guns. In fact, there were no guns—at least that's what Morrell claimed, and subsequent events supported him. But when the one-eyed warden appeared in Ed Morrell's solitary tomb, he wasn't looking for excuses. He wanted the guns, and he had brought a new tool to get them—the Overcoat, a heavy canvas straitjacket that was made not to restrain, but to torture:

> I had not been in it fifteen minutes, when pains began shooting through my fingers, hands and arms, gradually extending to my shoulders. Then over my whole body there was a prickling sensation like that of millions of sharp needles jabbing through the tender flesh.
>
> Next, a feeling of horror seized me. I must try to burst the canvas folds ere the devil's trap would choke out the last breath of life. . . .
>
> Hour after hour I endured the pain and as the time passed the anguish became more and more unbearable. . . .
>
> Now a new horror came. The bodily excretions over which I had no control in the canvas vice ate into my bruised limbs. My fingers, hands, and arms grew numb and dead.

Morrell's first session in the straitjacket lasted four days and fourteen hours. When he was released he was temporarily paralyzed; he then crawled to the straw tick bed and collapsed into a long, strange sleep. He heard voices, commanding him to perform daring feats and tests of bravery "like going through the rites of a weird initiation." In the final ordeal, he was led into a room where he saw everyone who had ever harmed him—the detective and gunmen who had hunted him down, the wardens, the prison guards, and stool pigeons—all being tortured themselves. It was a strange scene, but strangest of all was that he was filled with compassion. In his dream-like state he began to release them, one-by-one, freeing his enemies from the very tortures they had inflicted upon him.

Then he woke—or at least he opened his eyes—but he found himself flying through the prison walls, out into the sunlight, where he could see San Francisco Bay and the great glorious ocean beyond. He heard a voice, far away at first, but coming closer and closer until it seemed to be speaking in his ear. "You have learned the unreality of pain and hence of fear," said the voice. "You have learned the infutility of trying to fight your enemies with hatred. . . . From today a new life vista will open up . . . Your weapon will henceforth be the sword of love . . . even the straitjacket will have no terrors for you. It will only be a means to greater things. . . . Peace and love is yours!"

When Ed Morrell opened his eyes again he was in his dungeon cell. But everything was different, because he was different. "I was a new being," he recalled.

In the months that followed, Ed Morrell endured countless sessions with the canvas straitjacket, the longest lasting over five days. Each time, the warden ordered the guard to tie the jacket tighter in an effort to break his spirit. But the promise of the voice held true. The jacket could no longer contain him. After an initial period of horrible pain, his heart would seem to stop and he would feel his mind expanding, beyond the bounds of the canvas, beyond the walls of the prison, out into the infinite expanses of time and space. Today, we would call these experiences astral projection. Jack London called them "the little death." Ed Morrell preferred to call them "my new life in tune with a power divine."

On one of these astral journeys, Morrell saw a shipwreck in San Francisco Bay that he later discovered did indeed occur on the very day he lay in his straitjacket. On another occasion he managed to project himself into Jake Oppenheimer's cell, where he finally laid eyes on the pitiful wreck of a man with whom he had been communicating through the walls. But even more amazing were encounters with two people in the outside world who later played key roles in his life. One was a well-dressed, older gentleman in Alameda County, across the bay from San Quentin. The other was a blue-eyed schoolgirl in a town of central California.

The older gentleman entered his earthly life first. After a long session in the jacket, Morrell made a strange prediction to the brutal one-eyed warden. "This is the last time I will ever be tortured in the jacket! One year from today I will go out of this dungeon never to return to it; and better still, four years from the day I leave the dungeon I will walk from the prison a free man with a pardon in my hand. More, the governor of the state will bring that pardon in person to San Quentin!''

Sure enough—for reasons unknown—the one-eyed warden gave up on the jacket torture. A year later, in 1903, a new warden entered Ed Morrell's cell. In astonishment, the haggard, emaciated prisoner recognized him as the well-dressed, older man from Alameda County, a man he had never seen before in the material world. The new warden had made a full investigation of the hidden guns episode and found the charges to be unfounded. He ordered Ed Morrell released immediately from solitary confinement and returned to the prison population, where he installed him as "head trusty," the most powerful position a prisoner could hold. Morrell proved himself so capable in this position that in 1908—almost exactly as he had predicted—acting Governor Warren Porter of California personally delivered a full pardon to him at San Quentin.

As a free man, Ed Morrell devoted his life to a passionate plea for prison reform, moving audiences with first-hand accounts of the horrors behind prison walls. He addressed the legislatures of California and Pennsylvania and advised the U.S. Congress on the possibility of using inmates as soldiers during World War I. Although some considered him a wild-eyed idealist, he is credited by many as the father of the "honor system," which became the norm in American prisons. He was befriended and respected by many progressive thinkers of his day—from writer Jack London to Governor George Hunt of Arizona, who attested to the ex-convict's moral character in a foreword to Morrell's autobiography.

And what of the blue-eyed school girl of his astral wanderings? Morrell tried without success to find her in the town where he had seen her. Then one night he stopped at a house in San Francisco for yet another meeting on prison reform. A young woman of about eighteen answered the door, and Morrell instantly recognized her as the girl whom he had seen some six years earlier. She recognized him as well. "I have known you always," she told him later. "The moment I opened the door I recognized you as the man in stripes who came to me in a vision in the school room.''

Naturally they were married and lived happily ever after—a sweet coda to the strange case of Ed Morrell, the "Dungeon Man of San Quentin,'' who was saved for a higher purpose by a power divine.

JULY

To the scientific mind a miracle is an absurdity. But if its existence is observed under such conditions that there is no room left for any possibility of error it must be recognized as a fact. No argument can defeat the reality of a fact.

—DR. ALEXIS CARREL, *THE VOYAGE TO LOURDES*

A MIRACLE
IN THE GROTTO

As the train rattled through the French countryside, Dr. Alexis Carrel gently inserted a morphine-filled syringe into the withered arm of his young patient. "In five minutes the pain will be gone," he assured her.

The temporary relief of pain was all he could promise Marie Bailly. Ravaged by tubercular peritonitis—a cancerous inflammation of the abdominal lining—the young woman's body was a swollen mass of hard tumors and pockets of fluid. Her heartbeat and breathing were rapid and her temperature high. Dr. Carrel had grave doubts that she would survive this journey to Lourdes in search of a miracle.

It was July of 1903, forty-five years since a teenager named Bernadette claimed to have seen the Virgin Mary in the grotto of Lourdes. In that time, many cures had been credited to the waters of a spring that Bernadette had discovered. As a physician and a teacher of physicians, Dr. Carrel was intrigued by these reports. While most of his colleagues dismissed the Lourdes phenomena as nonsense, Carrel felt the cures deserved scientific investigation.

"It was a mistake to deny anything on the basis of laws which themselves were scarcely understood," he later wrote. "It was perfectly simple to examine the facts objectively, just as a patient was examined in a hospital or an experiment conducted in a laboratory. . . . if, by wild chance, the facts were true, it would be a signal opportunity to see something profoundly interesting."

For this reason, Carrel accepted an invitation to accompany a group of pilgrims on the train to Lourdes. It was essential that a physician be present on these journeys, for many of the patients were in such dangerous condition that the journey itself might prove fatal. Marie Bailly was not the only pilgrim who needed Dr. Carrel's attention during the long night on the train.

When the train arrived at Lourdes, Marie's nurse took her to Our Lady of the Seven Graces Hospital, while Dr. Carrel checked into a hotel. Later that day and again the next morning, he examined some of the patients at the hospital, including Marie Bailly, whose condition continued to deteriorate. These examinations were necessary in order to evaluate any reported cures scientifically, but for Alexis Carrel it was a sad, painful job. How could these sick, twisted bodies be cured by the waters?

Around noon, Dr. Carrel encountered an old classmate outside the hospital, where preparations were underway to take a new group of pilgrims to the grotto. His friend was working as a stretcher bearer, one of many volunteers who helped the sick to and from the healing pools. Having a little time before the afternoon session, the two men strolled through the town and had a cup of coffee. Carrel asked if anything unusual had happened that morning.

"I saw a miracle at the grotto," his friend replied. "I was walking near the pools when an old nun hobbled up on crutches. She let a little of the water run into a cup, made a large sign of the cross, and drank the water. Her whole face lighted with joy, she threw down her crutches, and almost ran to the grotto, where she kneeled before the Blessed Virgin. She was cured. I was told that, as a result of a sprain six months ago, she had developed an incurable disease in her foot."

Dr. Carrel was not impressed. "Her cure is an interesting example of autosuggestion. She happens to be one of the patients I examined." The sprain was very real, he explained, but it had actually healed by the time she arrived at Lourdes. The nun had convinced herself that she would never walk again, and that Lourdes offered the only hope. The healing was strictly psychological. The two men discussed various other claims of miraculous healings at Lourdes, but the well-trained doctor had explanations or doubts in every case.

"What kind of disease would you have to see cured," his friend finally asked, "to convince you that miracles exist?"

"An organic disease," Carrel replied. "A leg growing back after amputation, a cancer disappearing, a congenital dislocation suddenly vanishing." He thought of Marie Bailly, who had been so sick that morning that she had not yet been taken to the grotto. Dr. Carrel explained Marie's case in all its sad details to his friend. "She may die any moment right under my nose," he said. "If such a case as hers were cured, it would indeed be a miracle. I would never doubt again; I would become a monk!"

"Take care! Don't be too rash!" his friend laughed. "In Lourdes all the laws of nature are constantly turned upside down."

Dr. Carrel found his old classmate's simple faith touching, yet disturbing, for he realized that he had lost his own capacity to believe. His medical education had changed him fundamentally; he could only believe that which he could see, and touch, and measure.

An hour later, Carrel and his friend visited Marie in the hospital. Her condition was worse than ever. Her heart was racing erratically at 150 beats per minute, ready to give out at any time. Her entire body was swollen, and her stomach distended. Dr. Carrel could do little more to help her.

"Death is very near," he whispered to his friend.

Marie's nurse asked to take the young woman to the grotto, but Carrel was against it. In her condition, even the slightest movement might be enough to kill her. Another physician entered the ward, and Carrel asked him to corroborate the diagnosis. "She's at the point of death," the other doctor agreed. "She might very well die at the Grotto."

Overhearing the conversation, the Mother Superior of the hospital spoke up on Marie's behalf. "The girl has nothing to lose," she said. "It makes little difference whether she dies today or tomorrow. It would be cruel to deprive her of the supreme happiness of being taken to the Grotto, though I fear she may not live to reach it. We shall take her there now, in a few minutes."

Though Carrel doubted the wisdom of transporting the patient, he had no actual authority at the hospital. Besides, the Mother Superior was right—there was nothing to lose. So the two doctors went on to the grotto, while Carrel's old classmate attended to his duties as a stretcher bearer. A short while later, he and another volunteer carried Marie Bailly toward the pools. She was unconscious, and the bearers stopped for a moment to let Dr. Carrel take her pulse, which was racing more erratically than ever. Then they picked her up again and carried her toward the waters.

As he sat outside the pools, surrounded by so much physical misery, Alexis Carrel had a startling insight. He realized that Marie Bailly, about to die before she had a chance to live, was not truly unhappy because she believed in Christ and the Virgin Mary and a life after death. But he himself, a healthy man in the prime of his life, felt a deep unhappiness because he believed in nothing that he could not physically touch or see. Suddenly, spontaneously, for the first time in many years, Alexis Carrel began to pray, asking the Virgin Mary to heal Marie Bailly and to restore his own faith. The moment passed as quickly as it began, and he forced himself back into his scientific reverie.

Noticing that Marie had been carried from the pools, Carrel rushed over to examine her, but there was no change. She was exactly as he had expected her to be from a medical point of view. He couldn't help being a little disappointed. Marie's nurse reported that they had been afraid to immerse her in the water, so they had only poured a little on her distended abdomen. Now they were taking the dying patient to the grotto, where Bernadette had first seen the beautiful young woman in white.

Carrel remained for awhile with the other pilgrims, listening to the prayers of a priest and observing the faces of the sick. He could easily see how the environment of Lourdes would create a sense of rapture and ecstasy among these desperate people. He felt such emotions himself. But the emotional uplift of the experience could only have an effect on those whose diseases were emotional to begin with. Organic diseases were another matter.

Dr. Carrel walked toward the grotto with a young intern. There he found Marie Bailly lying on her stretcher in a special area reserved for the sick. "She was motionless," he later wrote, "her breathing still rapid and shallow; she seemed to be at the point of death." Turning away from Marie, Carrel watched other pilgrims crowding into the grotto. Many were desperately ill or hideously disfigured; others had come for purely spiritual reasons. When he glanced back at Marie, he was surprised to discover that her skin seemed less ashen, with a hint of color in her cheeks. He pointed this out to the intern, but the other replied skeptically, "All I can see is that she is no worse."

Carrel bent over the patient to take her pulse and listen to her breathing. "The respiration is less rapid," he said.

"That may mean that she is about to die," cautioned the intern.

Carrel concentrated all his attention on the patient. If something miraculous was really happening, he wanted to observe it scientifically, to note even the slightest details. Her face was clearly changing, her eyes opening wide in ecstasy. But there was more. "Look at her abdomen!" he shouted.

As the two doctors gazed in astonishment, the blanket covering Marie's swollen abdomen sank as though her body was healing before their eyes. Her heartbeat stabilized and she began to speak. "I feel well," she said, "I am still weak, but I feel I am cured." Moments later, Marie drank a cup of milk and raised her head to look around. She moved her arms and legs, and turned over onto her side—all without any apparent pain.

Overcome with emotion, Alexis Carrel jumped to his feet and walked off into the crowd. His entire world had been turned upside down. "There was no denying," he admitted, "that it was distressingly unpleasant to be personally involved in a miracle."

A few hours later, Dr. Carrel examined Marie in the hospital. She was sitting up in bed, and though she still showed the effects of her long illness, new life had returned to her face. Her pulse was a steady eighty beats per minute, half what it had been earlier that afternoon. Her breathing was slow and steady as well. But most miraculous of all, her abdomen appeared completely normal. There was no pain at his touch, no trace of the fluid and hard masses that had been so obvious in all his previous examinations. Doubting his sanity, Carrel asked three other physicians to examine her, but the diagnosis was unanimous. The dying girl had been cured—totally, spontaneously, and inexplicably in terms of any known physical process. Alexis Carrel had seen the very miracle he had said would convince him.

Despite his vow to "become a monk," Dr. Carrel continued his career as a physician, but with a new enthusiasm for the possibility of powers beyond the known physical world. When he returned from Lourdes, he reported what he had seen to his colleagues on the Faculty of Medicine at Lyons University, claiming that the events at Lourdes "prove the reality of certain links, as yet unknown between psychological and organic processes. They prove the objective value of the spiritual activity which has been almost totally ignored by doctors, teachers, and sociologists. They open up a new world for us."

Although these statements seem quite reasonable by the standards of the late twentieth century, Carrel was so vehemently attacked by his fellow physicians that he emigrated to the United States, where he worked at the University of Chicago and the Rockefeller Institute for Medical Research. While he never strayed from the scientific path, his belief in the power of miracles brought a new level of creativity to his research. In 1912, he received the Nobel prize in medicine for his pioneering work in vascular surgery and organ and tissue transplantation. The story of his visit to Lourdes was found among his papers when he died in 1944.

THE OIL DREAM

CRAWFORD COUNTY, ILLINOIS, IS LOCATED ABOUT 175 miles south of Chicago, nestled along the Wabash River that separates Illinois from Indiana. It's farm country— hogs, wheat, corn, and soybeans. But not so long ago, the rich, dark prairie soil yielded riches of another kind.

Back in 1908, a widow named Mrs. Weger lived in Crawford County, struggling to support herself and her children on an eighty acre farm. It was a hard life. She tried to send the children to school whenever she could, which meant whenever they had shoes and warm clothing. And she couldn't afford to hire help for the farm, so she had to do most of the farm work herself.

One night, Mrs. Weger had an unusually vivid dream. She saw herself sitting and crocheting in an elegant room with a piano, upholstered furniture, and an expensive Brussels carpet. Mrs. Weger enjoyed crocheting, but she never had time for it. Yet there she was in the dream, with all the leisure of a duchess.

In the following nights, Mrs. Weger dreamed the dream again. And again. The third time—while still in the dream—she set down her crocheting, stood up and walked out of the house. Outside, behind the henhouse, she saw a strange machine moving up and down. She had never seen a machine like that before, and she had no idea what it was.

Sometime later, Mrs. Weger saw an oil rig, and immediately recognized it as the strange machine in her dream. At that time, various companies were actively exploring for oil underneath the soil of Crawford County. When a drilling company offered to lease the mineral rights to her land, Mrs. Weger agreed—but she insisted that the lease agreement include a clause guaranteeing her the right to choose the location of the test well.

Mrs. Weger's farm was divided into eight ten-acre parcels, and the lease provided that, if the test well brought in oil, a well would be drilled on each parcel. When it came time to drill the test well, the assistant production superintendent—a man named Cramer—sent his drilling contractor, O'Mara, out to Mrs. Weger's farm, with orders to ask Mrs. Weger where to drive the stake to mark the well. But when O'Mara arrived, Mrs. Weger wasn't at home; she was out somewhere in the fields. Instead of looking for her, he just drove the stake in one of the corner parcels and guided his horse and buggy back to town.

At the company offices, O'Mara told Cramer what he had done, and the assistant superintendent insisted that they go back and find Mrs. Weger. The lease was very clear, and he wanted to follow it exactly. So Cramer and O'Mara got in the horse and buggy and rode the twelve miles out to the Weger farm. They found Mrs. Weger and asked her where to drive the stake. She showed them the spot behind the henhouse—the exact spot where she had seen the oil rig in her dream.

The test well struck oil, as did six other wells dug on the Weger farm. But the eighth well—drilled on the spot that O'Mara had originally marked for the test well—came up dry. If that well had been dug first, the lease would have been abandoned and the other wells would never have been drilled.

Mrs. Weger got her fine room with a piano, upholstered furniture, and an expensive Brussels carpet. Her children went to school everyday. And she had plenty of leisure time to crochet.

A Sound You
Never Forget

In the mid-1950s, Ernest Wilson bought land in Vista, California, a growing town between the ocean and inland valleys of San Diego County. A sturdy German immigrant in his late sixties, Wilson was a man of many talents—artistic and otherwise.

In his youth, he had traveled throughout the West with fellow artist Charles Russell, painting scenery for theaters along the way. Later he settled down to a career of teaching art. Now he planned to build his retirement dream house for himself and his wife, Gussie. But unlike most men his age—or most men of any age—when Ernest Wilson talked about building a house, he meant building it himself.

The land was mostly orange and avocado groves when they bought it, but there was a knoll that was perfect for a homesite. So Ernest and Gussie moved onto the land in a trailer and Ernest got to work on the construction project—with help from his son Harold and his teenage grandson, Willy.

First the three men cleared away the trees that covered the knoll. Then they built the garage, with a kitchen and temporary living quarters so Ernest and Gussie could move out of the trailer. Now work began on the house itself, with Ernest doing the hard physical labor of a much younger man. He seemed determined to outwork his son and grandson, and he had the strength and stamina to do it. One

127

day—just to show off—he wrapped one powerful hand around a beam in the unfinished house and proceeded to do one-handed pull-ups like they were the easiest thing in the world. Then he challenged his son and grandson to do the same. Harold managed a few, but Willy couldn't even pull himself up once. Ernest just shook his head and went back to work.

As a Christian Scientist, Ernest Wilson believed that good health was the natural order of God's creation. He carried his beliefs further as a Practitioner, a healer and leader of the congregation. It was said that Ernest had a special healing talent, and wherever he went, the local congregation grew. But it was the house in Vista that really put Ernest Wilson to the test.

One day, as the house neared completion, Ernest was working high on the roof, over twenty feet from the ground. Harold and Willy were downstairs doing the plumbing. They were just about to set a pipe into place—each holding one end—when they heard the horrible sound of Ernest falling from the roof.

"It was a sound you never forget," Willy says today. "You hear the ladder and *thunk!* . . . you just hear all the bones."

They dropped the pipe and raced out of the unfinished house to find Ernest bent back over a sawhorse, faceup toward the sky. It looked like his back was broken—maybe worse. "It wasn't natural," Willy remembers. "You just don't see that."

Harold and Willy lifted the older man carefully off the sawhorse, and pleaded with him to let them call a doctor. But he refused. "Just take me to my room," he whispered, "and give me my books."

So they carried Ernest into his room and left him with his Bible and his books of Christian Science philosophy. Then they went home and hoped for the best.

A few days later, they got a phone call. "I expected it to be my Grandma Gussie," Willy recalls, "telling us that my grandfather had died. But it wasn't Gussie. It was my grandfather saying, 'When are you guys coming back to work?' We went back the next day and picked up where we left off. I never noticed any ill effects at all.''

To Christian Scientists, a healthy body is the natural order of God's creation and it's only human error that allows us to believe we are sick or injured. But to fall from the top of a house, to land bent backward over a sawhorse, and then—without medical care—to return to work as if nothing happened a few days later certainly seems miraculous. Just ask Willy Wilson, the teenage boy who saw it happen.

Willy has grandchildren of his own now, but he remembers his grandfather's remarkable recovery as clearly as if it were yesterday. "It sure seemed like a miracle to me."

THE WOMAN WHO DIDN'T EAT

In July 1927, four nuns arrived at the home of the Neumann family in Konnersreuth, a small Bavarian town near the border between Germany and Czechoslovakia. The nuns were nursing sisters working under the supervision of a highly respected physician named Dr. Seidl, who had been appointed by the local bishop to investigate the case of Theresa Neumann. At that time, Theresa was twenty-nine years old, and she had already lived one of the strangest lives in the annals of mystical literature.

Born on Good Friday of 1898, Theresa grew up to be a simple, cheerful, and robust young woman. As a teenager, she worked on a neighbor's farm, where she did a man's share of the labor while most of the men were away fighting in World War I. Then, in March 1918, a fire broke out on another nearby farm, and Theresa joined the bucket brigade trying to douse the flames. In the midst of her efforts, a pail slipped from her hands, and she was unable to continue, complaining of numbness in her legs and a pinching pain in her back. For a time she did only lighter tasks around the farm, but in April her employer forced her to resume heavy work. Shortly afterward, as she was carrying a sack of potatoes up the stairs from the cellar, her legs collapsed beneath her and she slipped and fell backward, hitting her head on a stone ledge.

After the blow to her head, Theresa's personality

changed dramatically. She became extremely irritable and unreasonable, and suffered what were apparently epileptic seizures. Although she had the best medical care that her parents could afford, her condition only worsened, and in May 1919, she came out of a convulsive attack to discover she was blind. She also developed a variety of problems on the left side of her body: loss of feeling, paralysis in the arm, and deafness.

Up to this point there was nothing truly remarkable about Theresa's physical condition. She obviously injured her back while fighting the fire, and the back injury affected her legs, which caused her to collapse under the weight of the potatoes. The blow to her head then caused the personality changes and the seizures. The blindness, deafness, paralysis, and loss of feeling can also be explained as physical or psychosomatic results of the injuries. But around Christmas 1922, Theresa's life began to enter uncharted territory. She experienced a strange pain in her throat that made it impossible for her to swallow solid food. From then on, she stopped eating, though she continued to receive communion every day and—for a time—to drink sustaining liquids.

From an early age, Theresa had felt a special spiritual connection with Thérèse of Lisieux, a young French nun who died the year before Theresa Neumann was born, and this connection apparently opened the path of healing. On April 29, 1925, the day that Thérèse of Lisieux was beatified, the second step toward Catholic sainthood, Theresa Neumann was cured of her blindness. On May 17 of the same year, Thérèse of Lisieux was canonized a Catholic saint, and Theresa Neumann recovered from paralysis. On September 10, the anniversary of St. Thérèse's death, Theresa Neumann was able to leave her bed unaided and resume her daily activities.

Because Theresa Neumann's original afflictions may have been psychosomatic, it's difficult to know whether her recovery was truly miraculous, though it certainly seemed that way to her at the time. But the miracles were only beginning.

On the night of March 4, 1926, Theresa had a vision of Christ kneeling and praying in the Garden of Gethsemane. When the figure turned to look at her, she felt a sharp pain in her left side, just above the heart, and noticed blood flowing down from the area of the pain. This was the beginning of her stigmata, a sharing of the physical wounds that Christ suffered on the cross. During the following weeks, Theresa developed wounds in her hands and feet as well. In November, eight smaller wounds broke out around her forehead, mimicking the crown of thorns. Later, another wound developed in her shoulder, and she also bled from her eyes.

With bizarre regularity, Theresa's wounds opened and bled on Fridays, while she entered a trance-like state and saw visions of Christ's Passion—the events leading up to and including the crucifixion. Theresa saw the Passion not as a continuous vision, but as a series of short scenes, like the traditional Stations of the Cross. She also saw many events not mentioned in the Gospels. In the periods between visions, her mind seemed to function like that of a very small child, but during the visions she spoke with powerful authority, using complex words and phrases. After the "Friday ecstasies," the wounds would heal, only to open again on another Friday.

Around Christmas 1926, Theresa Neumann stopped drinking liquid for nourishment. Her entire physical intake was now a daily communion wafer with a swallow of water. Actually, she could only partake of a full wafer when she was in the midst of ecstasy; the rest of the time she could only swallow a tiny piece, perhaps an eighth of the wafer.

By this time, news of Theresa's stigmata and inedia (noneating) had spread far beyond her little town, and the bishop of the region appointed an official commission to investigate the situation—which brings us back to the four nuns who arrived in July 1927. Theresa's father had agreed to a two-week period of strict medical observation, and the nuns had instructions from the supervising physician to watch Theresa constantly, measuring everything that entered and left her body.

The results of this two-week test are fascinating. On the simplest level, the nuns confirmed that Theresa Neumann did indeed go for two weeks without ingesting anything except the communion wafer and a swallow of water each day. The lack of food is not unusual in itself, because a human being can easily fast for that period of time; however the lack of water is more difficult to explain. But most remarkable is that Theresa lost weight during her Friday ecstasies and then gained it back over the next few days, all without eating or drinking anything of nutritional value. On Wednesday, July 13—the night before the test officially began—Theresa weighed fifty-five kilograms (121 pounds). On the following Saturday, her weight had dropped to fifty-one kilograms (approximately 112 pounds), but it was back up to fifty-four kilograms (approximately 119 pounds) by Wednesday. The pattern was repeated the following week, and on the final day, Thursday, July 28, she once again weighed fifty-five kilograms, exactly as she had at the beginning of the experiment.

Two months later, on September 30, 1927, Theresa Neumann stopped taking water with her daily communion wafer. She lived for thirty-five more years without eating or drinking, and, except when suffering from her Friday ecstasies, enjoyed an astonishingly active life, attending church, visiting the sick, and helping her family with household chores. Photographs show a robust, almost plump woman with a round, smiling face. Theresa Neumann died on September 18, 1962. That morning, for the first time in many years, she had asked for a little water with her communion wafer.

Unfortunately—though understandably—Theresa and her family refused to allow further periods of strict measurement and experimentation, but she was observed by many doctors and other reliable individuals over the years, and no one ever saw any indication that she broke her total fast. Although invariably cheerful and polite to those who came to visit her, Theresa became frustrated with the constant medical scrutiny, because she believed that scientific experts missed the point of her life. In a letter to a friend, Theresa wrote, "I always think that true science and knowledge are supposed to lead to our dear God, but the contrary is usually the case. . . . I do not know how these people who keep torturing me, like the doctors, can have such a poor grasp of the fact that God can do more things than they can understand."

What was the point of Theresa's life? Or more specifically, what was the point of her life without food and drink? Jesuit scholar Herbert Thurston, who wrote about Theresa's case in 1931, expressed the fundamental strangeness of the whole issue quite clearly: "After all, one asks, what higher purpose does the demonstration of this inedia serve? The Almighty cannot wish us to conclude that pious Christians, encouraged by Theresa's example, should strive to live without eating. Abstemiousness carried to this excess would not be virtue, but a vice—a tempting of God."

Thurston never answers his own question, and I'm not sure I can answer it either. However, it seems to me that perhaps the message of Theresa Neumann's life is that even the most basic physical human needs—eating and drinking—are not truly needs if God so wills it. In the end, we are not creatures of the physical world, but of a better world, the world of the spirit.

For other stories of stigmata, see "The Wounds of St. Francis" in September and "Tears, Blood, and Father Jim" in November.

OH . . .
THERE HE IS

THOMAS ATTENDED BARD COLLEGE, A SMALL AND PRES-
tigious liberal arts school in upstate New York. Like most
small colleges, it is a breeding ground for deep and lasting
friendships, a place where like-minded young people find
connection in a shared curiosity and lust for life. Thomas's
own group of friends, he admits, were a bit outside the
mainstream. "We were a degenerate bunch," he writes today, "artists, poets, European alcoholics, and neo-tribal
types. Nothing had the power to divide the unspoken love
we had for one another, though we fought and argued and
mocked one another unceasingly."

Most of the group were men, with women filtering in
and out as they formed or broke off relationships with the
men. But one woman was different. Her name was Laura,
and she was "one of the guys" from the beginning—
though she was a whole lot prettier than they were.

In late spring 1991, the school year came to an end and
the group went their separate ways, so sure they'd see each
other soon that their good-byes didn't seem real at all. Thomas got Laura's summer address, but he couldn't give her
his because he didn't know it. All he knew was that he
would be spending the summer in South Dakota, working
under a program called Partnership for Service Learning.

After Thomas arrived in South Dakota, he was placed
with the American Indian Services in Sioux Falls and as-

signed to help organize the Northern Plains Tribal Arts show. The program provided a room for him in a local hotel that he succinctly describes as "a dump." Although the work itself was interesting, Sioux Falls was not exactly a booming metropolis and it was a long way from his family in Georgia and his friends in New York. Thomas soon found himself feeling lonely and depressed, like a soldier stuck in a desolate outpost.

Thomas wrote to Laura early in the summer—before he received his job placement—describing his loneliness and giving her his address. But though she received and read the letter, she lost the envelope. That July, Laura and her roommate Stacy decided to drive from New York to California. Sioux Falls was right on the way, so they stopped off in the city, hoping to find Thomas. It was kind of a crazy idea, really. Sioux Falls isn't exactly New York or Chicago, but it's still a big city. They didn't have an address, there was no telephone listing, and they didn't know where he was working.

Actually Thomas wasn't working that day, anyway, and he wasn't even in Sioux Falls. It was a Saturday, and he had gone to a powwow in the small town of Flandreau, about forty miles to the north. He hadn't told anyone about his plans; he just woke up that morning and decided to go.

When Laura and Stacy realized that there was no way they'd ever find Thomas in Sioux Falls, they got back in the car and continued on their way to California. But instead of heading straight west, they decided to travel north for a while and then continue westward through Montana and Idaho. About forty miles out of Sioux Falls, they made a pitstop for gas, a bathroom break, and a cold drink. As they were driving out of the gas station, they happened to notice a posterboard sign tacked onto a telephone pole: POWWOW 3 MILES →

"Wanna go see it?" Laura asked Stacy.

"Sure," Stacy replied. And so they did.

At the powwow, Thomas thought it strange when he felt a pair of arms wrap around him from behind. But when he turned and saw Laura with a big grin on her face, he thought he was hallucinating. "Laura?" he asked.

"I've come to save you, Thomas," she replied. Yes, she was real. She spoke and smiled and laughed.

For Thomas it was a day of pure, unadulterated joy, a shot of love and friendship that got him through the long, lonely summer. "I have always ascribed this event to divine intervention," he writes today. "The odds are almost incalculable. Miracles do not get any more joyous than that day was."

For Laura, however, the experience had a strangely natural quality, as if she had been led to Thomas all along. When she first saw him standing at the powwow, she thought, *Oh . . . there he is*, as if it were the most natural thing in the world. And perhaps it was natural—in a world where we are guided by the spirit as much as by signs on telephone poles.

AUGUST

We have been told by the white men, or at least those who are Christian, that God sent to men His son, who would restore order and peace upon the earth; and we have been told that Jesus the Christ was crucified, but that he shall come again at the Last Judgment, the end of this world cycle.

This I understand and know that it is true, but the white men should know that for the red people too, it was the will of Wakan-Tanka, the Great Spirit, that an animal turn itself into a two-legged person in order to bring the most holy pipe to His people; and we too were taught that this White Buffalo Cow Woman who brought our sacred pipe will appear again at the end of the "world," a coming which we Indians know is now not very far off.

—BLACK ELK, *THE SACRED PIPE*

A BUFFALO NAMED MIRACLE

IN THE EARLY MORNING HOURS OF AUGUST 20, 1994, just before dawn, a female white buffalo calf was born on an exotic animal farm in Janesville, Wisconsin. The owners of the farm, Dave and Valerie Heider, named the buffalo Miracle—for the birth of a white buffalo is so rare that it's almost supernatural, and American Indians hold the white buffalo sacred.

Back in the days of the great herds, when some sixty million buffalo roamed the North American Plains, the odds of a true white, non-albino buffalo calf being born were approximately one in ten million. Today, the odds are impossible to calculate. The herd was reduced to less than a thousand animals in the late nineteenth century, and though the number has now risen to almost 200,000, no one knows how many of the tiny, late nineteenth century herd carried the recessive gene that produces a white coat.

White buffalo calves are occasionally reported to the American Bison Association, but they are either albinos— a trait that occurs in all animals—or a cross between a buffalo and a cow, which sometimes produces a lighter coat. Miracle is not an albino, for her eyes are brown rather than pink. And she is the offspring of two buffaloes. By the spring of 1995, her permanent coat had begun to come in, showing a slight darkening around the face, neck, and legs. But that doesn't change the fact that she was born white, the only recorded birth of a true white female buffalo calf. The last white buffalo was a male with a brown topnotch, who was born in 1933 and died in 1959.

But Miracle is far more than a genealogical oddity. For the American Indian people, she is a harbinger of a new age, a symbol that the time has come for humanity to unite in peace and harmony. Within days, Indian visitors came from near and far to pay their respects to the white calf. One of them, a Lakota medicine man named Floyd Hand, explained, "This is like the second coming of Christ on this island of North America. The legend is she would return and unify the nations of the four colors—the black, red, yellow, and white."

"She" is White Buffalo Calf Woman, a being sacred to the Lakota and many other Indian tribes. According to Lakota legend, long ago the people came together to camp and hunt, but there was no game to be found. A chief named Standing Hollow Horn sent out two warriors to hunt, and as they stood upon a hill they saw a beautiful woman walking toward them in a sacred manner, clothed in white buckskin and carrying a bundle on her back. She was so beautiful that one of the warriors was overcome with desire, but the other warrior warned him that such thoughts were impure, for she was a sacred woman.

When the woman drew nearer, she motioned to the lustful warrior to approach her. The two were enveloped in a great cloud, and when the cloud lifted, the lustful warrior was nothing but a pile of bones. The woman then ordered the pious warrior to go back to his camp and ask the chief to prepare a large tipi for her coming, saying, "I wish to tell you something of great importance!"

When White Buffalo Calf Woman appeared at the camp, she opened her bundle to reveal the sacred pipe. Holding the stem in her right hand and the bowl in her left, she explained that the pipe represented the earth and all that lived upon it. When the people smoked this pipe in prayer, all the things of the earth sent their voices upward to *Wakan-Tanka*, the Great Spirit. "When you pray with this pipe," she said, "you pray for and with everything."

White Buffalo Calf Woman taught the Lakota other things as well, including the first of seven great rituals that would form the heart of their religious worship, promising that the other rituals would be revealed in time. When she was finished, she said, "Remember, in me there are four ages. I am leaving now, but I shall look back upon your people in every age, and at the end I shall return." As she walked away, the mysterious woman turned into a white buffalo calf and disappeared.

Is Miracle, the calf in Janesville, Wisconsin, truly the second coming of White Buffalo Calf Woman, the fulfillment of the prophecy? Does her birth signify the end of the four ages—the present cycle of earthly existence—and the beginning of a new age of peace and harmony? Only time will tell, but for the thousands of pilgrims who have journeyed to the Heider farm, the little calf is indeed a miracle.

AN OPENING
IN THE CLOUDS

Letty and Katy were as close as a mother and daughter could be. Letty had divorced Katy's father when the girl was not quite two years old, and for the next ten years the two lived together in blissful harmony, growing and exploring the world together. Letty completed her education and found a good job as a school librarian, which provided for their material needs and gave her time to spend with her daughter. Katy still saw her father occasionally, but he was never there for her the way her mother was. It was always Letty and Katy.

Then Letty met Jack, a strong, solid man with two boys of his own—one the same age as Katy, the other a few years younger. Letty and Jack married in 1983, two months before Katy's twelfth birthday. Suddenly, the close relationship between mother and daughter was threatened. After ten years of giving Katy her undivided attention, Letty had to spread her energies around, giving of herself to her husband and her two new sons, as well as to her daughter. At the same time, Katy found herself face-to-face with a man who was willing to handle the responsibilities of fatherhood that her own father had avoided. Jack's sons had trouble adjusting, too, and though the children tried to get along, there were some pretty rocky times. It definitely wasn't The Brady Bunch.

Unfortunately for Katy, this upheaval came just as she

was entering the first stages of adolescence. An early bloomer, she was soon looking for happiness outside the home—in boys and drugs. At fifteen she began to run away, and at sixteen she left home for good, moving in with a drug dealer. Letty was heartbroken. In a few short years, she had lost her precious daughter. They couldn't even talk anymore.

In August 1989, Letty was busy preparing for the beginning of the school year. By this time, Katy had been gone for a year and a half, but the boys were still at home, and Letty's mother offered to come and help out for a few days. Letty's parents, Helen and Johnie, lived in northeastern Oklahoma, a four-hour drive from Letty's home in Norman. Although they were both in their mid-seventies, they had always been in excellent health and were still active, vital people.

Suddenly, on the Sunday before she was planning to leave for Norman, Helen got very ill. She had no idea what was wrong; she just felt weak and horrible. She decided to rest for a couple of days and see if she could kick it, but by Wednesday she was so sick that she couldn't even get off the couch. The next day, her husband took her to the local hospital, where the doctors discovered that she had a life-threatening, generalized infection called sepsis. The infection was especially hard on the respiratory system, and on Friday afternoon, in the midst of a procedure to aid her breathing, a young doctor mistakenly deflated her lungs. Now Helen was rushed to the Intensive Care Unit at St. Francis Hospital in Tulsa.

That evening, Letty came home to find a note from her oldest stepson, Michael, telling her that there was a family emergency and he had gone to get his father. The note explained that she should call their neighbor to find out the details. To Letty, this was a small miracle in itself, for Michael had never demonstrated that level of responsibility before, and he had never shown any concern for her. But now he was rising to the occasion. When Letty called the neighbor and got the full report, she realized that there was another young person who needed to rise to the occasion as well—Katy.

Letty went to Katy's house and told her that Grandma was very sick and that she wanted her to come to Tulsa. Without a word of argument, Katy grabbed a few things and joined her mother and stepfather for the two-hour trip. Along the way, sitting in the car with the daughter who seemed so lost, Letty thought about her own relationship with her mother. They had never been really close, at least not the way that Letty and Katy had once been. Letty had been much closer to her father, Johnie. He was a golf pro, and she had just turned pro herself, following in his footsteps. But as for her mother, well, she always thought there would be time to forge a deeper relationship. Now it seemed that time was running out.

When they arrived at the hospital late Friday night, Letty was shocked by what she saw; the woman in the hospital bed didn't look like her mother at all. She was misshapen and bloated, pumped full of air in a desperate effort to reinflate her lungs. She couldn't speak and barely recognized her family. All that was keeping her alive were the tubes, wires, and machines of the Intensive Care Unit. Letty could see that the situation was hopeless, and she would have preferred that Helen be taken off the life-support systems. But her father wanted the medical staff to keep his beloved wife alive as long as they could. So the four of them—Johnie, Letty, Jack, and Katy—passed a long, weary night, first in a large waiting room with other families of intensive care patients, then in a smaller, private room reserved for the families of patients who were about to die.

Around nine in the morning, they walked down the hall to check on Helen in the ICU. But just as they were about to enter the outer door, Letty heard the medical team shouting, "Code Blue," the hospital code for cardiac arrest. Instinctively, she knew it was her mother, and she didn't want her father to see the intense, invasive procedures that would follow. So she gently led him back to the private waiting room, tears welling in his eyes. It was hard for her to see her father cry; he'd always been so strong and good-natured, so affable and downright happy. Sensing his wife's discomfort, Jack stepped in and led Johnie to another corner of the room, offering his own form of man-to-man solace.

Now Letty and Katy stood together, looking out the window. It had been raining all morning, and the sky was a solid gray blanket of clouds. There was a golf course across the street from the hospital, and Letty thought how appropriate it was—she and her father had spent half their lives on golf courses.

Suddenly, a space opened up in the clouds, and the morning sun came streaming through, shining on the hospital wall and illuminating part of the golf course, though it continued to rain all around the shaft of sunlight. Letty smiled at the beautiful display of the natural world. But then she saw something else, something beyond what we call nature. Emerging out of the hospital building to her left, just outside the Intensive Care Unit, Letty saw her mother rising on the shaft of sunlight. She looked beautiful and healthy and young, dressed in a black skirt and a white blouse, her hair in the blonde curls she had worn when Letty was a child. As Letty continued to watch, her mother rose until she disappeared through the opening in the clouds. Then the clouds closed and the sunlight was gone.

For a moment Letty struggled with disbelief. Her brain said that what she had seen was impossible, or at best an illusion. But her heart told her it was absolutely real, as real as the rain falling on the golf course. She decided to trust her heart.

"Grandma's gone," she said softly, turning to Katy, who was standing a few feet to her right.

"I know," Katy replied. "I just saw her leave."

Letty stared at her daughter. "What did you see?" she asked.

"Grandma looked so beautiful. She just floated up into the sky."

For a long while, mother and daughter stood together in silence, looking out the window. "Nothing broke the magic of the moment," Letty remembers today. "It was our moment. It was peaceful. We were almost smiling on the inside.''

A few minutes later, the doctor arrived to tell them that Helen had died. It was heartbreaking for Johnie, heartbreaking for all of them. But for Letty and Katy it was also the beginning of a new relationship, a shaft of sunlight shining through the clouds of pain and anger that had separated them. During the funeral arrangements Katy was there for Letty, returning home to pack for the whole family, taking care of responsibilities that she would have run from in the past. She still had a long way to go and rocky times waited ahead, but that August morning Katy found a new inner strength and a new relationship with her mother.

As I write this in March 1995, Katy has been drug-free for over three years. She's a responsible twenty-three-year-old woman, who lives on her own and supports herself with a good job. She is fully reconciled with Letty, and their relationship is closer and deeper than ever. Perhaps that is the real miracle of the story—the reunion of mother and daughter. But it began when they both saw a woman they loved, rising on a shaft of sunlight, leaving this life through an opening in the clouds.

PROBLEMS
OF THE HEART

In August 1984, Alexander Rohow had a heart attack while working as an electrician in the Chicago area. A sixty-year-old Russian immigrant, Rohow underwent triple bypass surgery and began the long, slow period of recovery. Although he didn't know it, someone else—someone very close to him—was going through a similar ordeal on the other side of the world.

Over forty years earlier, when Germany invaded Russia during World War II, Alexander had been separated from his family. Originally sent to a work camp in the Rhineland, he was later forced to serve in the German Army. When the war ended, Alexander was shuffled from one refugee camp to another, and in 1950, at a camp in Austria, he met another refugee named Nelly. They married and their daughter Elsa was born in Austria in 1953. Two years later, with help from a special fund set up by the daughter of Russian writer Leo Tolstoy, they emigrated to the United States, where they had a son and began a new life in their adopted country.

Though Alexander Rohow prospered in America, a heavy sadness enveloped his heart. He had completely lost touch with his family—his parents and his three brothers. What had become of them? To Alexander it seemed as if they had been blown away like leaves on the wind. And in the strict secrecy of the Cold War, it was impossible to

149

discover where they had come to rest behind the Iron Curtain.

Then in late 1991, the Soviet Union collapsed and the Iron Curtain opened to the world. For the first time, Alexander had hope that he might be able to locate his family. Nelly had been corresponding with her own family for some time, and she had managed to discover a single lead to her husband's past: the address of a cousin in Russia. Alexander and Nelly wrote to the cousin and asked if he knew of anyone in the Rohow family. The cousin replied with the address of Viktor Rohow in Siberia. Viktor was Alexander's brother!

Now—after a half century of silence—an extraordinary flow of letters began to pass back and forth between Alexander in Chicago and Viktor in Siberia. For the first time, Alexander discovered what had happened to his parents and his other brothers, how and where they had died. But it was the living brother who touched him most. Alexander had so much to say to Viktor, so much to try and explain. He would tear his letters up again and again, trying to get them just right, until Nelly had to step in and write them for him.

Viktor's wife, Masha, also had to write the letters, but for a different reason. Viktor Rohow had suffered a massive stroke in 1984, the same year that Alexander had his heart attack and triple bypass surgery. Two brothers—two problems of the heart—separated by half a century and half the world. While Alexander had recovered from his heart problem, Viktor had not. He was partially paralyzed and could barely walk. He had severe memory loss, and though he tried to scribble out his own words in the letters to his brother in America, he didn't have enough muscle control to write. So Masha wrote for him . . . at first.

As the flow of letters continued, however, Masha reported a remarkable change in her husband. He sat and read Alexander's letters over and over again, with tears in his eyes, but through the tears he gained strength. Little by little, Viktor Rohow began to walk, to regain the muscle control that he had lost almost a decade earlier. His memory returned, and soon he was writing the letters himself, in a strong flowing hand that spoke boldly and lovingly across the space and time that separated him from his brother.

Today, Viktor Rohow has completely recovered from the stroke that left him debilitated for over eight years. The doctors in Siberia believe that it was the joyous "shock" of discovering his long-lost brother that set him on the road to his remarkable healing. But perhaps there is an even deeper explanation. Some healers believe that physical disease is a manifestation of an underlying emotional or spiritual problem. Alexander and Viktor Rohow lived their lives with broken hearts, mourning the loss of their family connection. They suffered heart problems at the same time, separated by half the world. And it was only when they found each other again that both their hearts were healed.

CARRIED TO THE CEILING

In August 1852, a wealthy silk merchant named Ward Cheney held a séance at his home in Connecticut. This was during the fascination with Spiritualism that swept the upper levels of American and European society in the mid-nineteenth century. Cheney had invited a nineteen-year-old medium named Daniel Dunglas Home to create the usual séance effects of spirit rapping, moving tables, and mysterious lights. But young D. D. Home did something more unusual—something no one expected, including Home himself.

The son of a solid Scottish carpenter and a clairvoyant mother, Home's spiritual powers manifested early—a relative even claimed that his cradle rocked by itself. At the age of four he predicted the death of a cousin, and at thirteen he accurately "saw" a friend's death far away. In the meantime, his family moved from Scotland to Connecticut. After his mother died in 1850, Home lived with his aunt, who became convinced that the strange rappings in her house were the result of her nephew's demonic possession. She called in Christian ministers to drive out the evil spirits, but the ministers believed that young D. D. Home had a God-given gift.

At the séance in the home of the silk merchant, the gift manifested itself full-force. One of the guests was F. L. Burr, a skeptical newspaper editor from the *Hartford Times*.

His written report is the best description we have of the event:

> Suddenly, without any expectation on the part of the company, Home was taken up into the air. I had hold of his hand at the time and I felt his feet—they were lifted a foot from the floor. He palpitated from head to foot with the contending emotions of joy and fear which choked his utterances. Again and again he was taken from the floor, and the third time he was carried to the ceiling of the apartment, with which his hands and feet came into gentle contact.

News of the levitation spread quickly, and D. D. Home became the most famous medium of the nineteenth century, perhaps the most famous medium of all time. In 1855, he returned to his native Europe where he was honored by royalty and high society for almost two decades. Home held at least 1,500 recorded séances during his long career, all in the light, and no one ever caught him in obvious fraud. In many of those séances he was seen to levitate by otherwise rational observers, including Emperor Napoleon III and British social critic John Ruskin.

Home never charged for his performances, but relied instead on the generosity of his wealthy patrons. He derided most mediums as fakes, and attributed his own powers to "friendly spirits." Along with levitation, Home performed a variety of other feats, including shrinking and stretching his body, carrying red-hot coals without getting burned, and producing ghostly hands that shook the outstretched hands of startled humans. But it is the levitations that seem most intriguing, even a century and a half later. Home described the experience in clear and strangely believable terms:

> I feel no hands supporting me, and, since the first time, I have never felt fear; though should I have fallen from the ceiling of some rooms in which I have been raised, I could not have escaped serious injury. I am generally lifted up perpendicularly; my arms frequently become rigid, and are

drawn above my head, as if I were grasping an unseen power which slowly raises me from the floor.

In 1871, Home submitted his powers to a series of tests by the great British scientist Sir William Crookes. Crookes was a highly respected chemist and physicist, who discovered the element thallium and invented the radiometer and cathode-ray tube, the latter research playing a key role in the discoveries of X rays and electrons. After the death of his brother, he developed an interest in Spiritualism and risked his scientific reputation to study psychic phenomena. To William Crookes, it seemed that these phenomena were not that far removed from the unseen forces he studied in his mainstream scientific work.

Under controlled scientific conditions, Crookes observed Home levitate and display other paranormal powers. One of Home's most famous séance "tricks" was to make an accordion play without touching it. Crookes hypothesized that Home manipulated electromagnetic waves in order to accomplish this. So in an effort to block this manipulation, the scientist wrapped an accordion in copper wire, placed it in a wire cage, and ran electricity through the wires. D. D. Home still made the accordion play without touching it.

When Crookes published the results of his tests, he suggested that Home's powers derived from some unknown "psychic force," rather than spirits. By the standards of twentieth century parapsychology, this seems a reasonable hypothesis, but in the less tolerant climate of Victorian England, Crookes was subjected to hostile ridicule from the scientific community. One of his critics suggested that the phenomena he reported could not have happened, for the simple reason that they were impossible.

"I never said it was possible," Crookes replied, "I only said it was true." A fitting epitaph, perhaps, for the remarkable career of Daniel Dunglas Home.

WHO IS
THIS BROTHER,
ANYWAY?

*In 1971, Michael D. was twice saved by a voice in his
head, warning him of his wife's imminent efforts to kill
him. The story of the voice is told in "Wake Up!" in January. Eleven years later, Michael met the man behind
the voice.*

In 1982, MICHAEL D. WORKED AS AN ACUPUNCTURIST IN
Chicago, specializing in helping people detoxify themselves
from drug habits. At the same time, he was also dealing
drugs. As Michael admits today with a self-deprecating
smile, "I had both ends of the business covered."

Searching for further training, he decided to study acu-
puncture in Sri Lanka, the island nation off the coast of
southern India. Not surprisingly, considering his double
lifestyle in Chicago, Michael also viewed the trip as a good
opportunity to get high. He'd heard there were some powerful drugs in Asia.

In Sri Lanka, Michael happened to visit some people
who had pictures of an Indian holy man displayed in their
home. As Michael—an African American—gazed at the
kinky-haired, brown-skinned guru, he wondered, *Who is
this brother, anyway?* He asked his host about the pictures
and discovered the man was Sai Baba, a religious leader
who had an ashram in southern India. Michael decided to

visit the ashram. He couldn't really explain why. He just felt he should do it.

On Friday, August 13, 1982, Michael D. arrived at Sai Baba's ashram, *Prashanti Nilayam,* which means "Abode of the Highest Peace." With hundreds of other people, he gathered for *darshan,* a daily ritual in which the guru appears before his followers. When Sai Baba entered the *darshan* area, Michael found himself thinking, *I just want to make eye contact with this guy.* Suddenly, Sai Baba rose and walked through the crowd directly toward him. Without speaking a word, the guru thrust his face toward Michael's and glared directly into his eyes.

Later, Michael joined a dozen other people for a group interview with Sai Baba, watching in fascination as the guru materialized a variety of objects out of the air: food, a strand of prayer beads, sacred ash. So far, Michael was amazed by all he had experienced at the ashram. But the real amazement began when he was granted a private interview with Sai Baba. This was a special privilege, for there were always hundreds—and often thousands—of people at the ashram, and it would be impossible for the guru to meet with each of them individually.

As soon as Michael was alone with Sai Baba, he realized that this was the man whose voice had saved him eleven years earlier . . . the man who had ordered him to "Wake up!" in time to see his wife approaching with a loaded .30 caliber carbine . . . the man who had told him to "Wake up!" again, in time to find his wife boiling hot oil on the stove, in preparation for another attack.

"It wasn't really his voice that I recognized," Michael says today. "It was his being, his presence. I just knew it was him."

Later, in another private interview, Sai Baba confirmed that it was indeed he who spoke to Michael during the violent end of his marriage, revealing details of the situation that no one else would know. But in this first interview, the guru had something more immediate to discuss.

"Too much lust!" he shouted, startling his American visitor. "Sometimes you want to be with Mary. Sometimes you want to be with all these other women.''

Michael gazed at the holy man in amazement. It was true. Several months before leaving Chicago, he had broken up with a steady girlfriend named Mary and thrown himself full force into a wild life of sexual excess. He'd only been at the ashram a short time, and he hadn't discussed his past with anyone. How did Baba know?

As the interview continued, Michael discovered that Baba knew many other things about him—more than he knew himself. Baba knew his struggles and his fears. Baba knew that he was caught between the path of healing and the path of self-destruction. But most importantly of all, Baba promised to guide him. "I'll help you," he said.

After six days, Michael left the ashram and checked into a hotel in the nearby city of Bangalore. As soon as he was settled into his room, he remembers, "I proceeded to freak. I was pacing back and forth, going crazy. My whole value system had been turned upside down." Trying to come to grips with himself, Michael sat down and scribbled some thoughts in his journal:

> This is so immense, it approaches being incomprehensible. The significance of this last week is overwhelming. Praise be to God! This is the task I've dreamed of, the spiritual salvation of Mankind. . . .

When he looked at what he had just written, it seemed even more incomprehensible and overwhelming. Here he was—Michael D., drug dealer, ladies' man and professional pleasure seeker—writing about the spiritual salvation of Mankind! He felt as if he were split through the heart. A part of him really did want to change and do something more meaningful and spiritually significant, but another part—the lazy part—resisted the change, thinking, *I want to get back to the old Mike.*

Michael decided to put on some music to drown out his inner argument. He grabbed a tape by the reggae group Third World, and shoved it into the Sony Walkman he carried with him on his travels. The first song was "Try Jah

Love." Though he'd listened to it countless times before, he'd never paid attention to the words, only to the beat and the melody. But now the lyrics jumped out at him like a reminder of what he'd just experienced at the ashram. The song tells the story of a "lonely soul" who discovers God's unconditional love.

Michael didn't want to hear about it. He turned off the music and decided to smoke a joint. Most people smoke pot to get high, but Michael figured it would bring him down—down to the reality of his old life, down to the old Mike. He stepped out on the balcony of his hotel room and began to roll the joint. He'd done it so many times before that he didn't have to watch his hands, so he gazed up absently into the sky.

"Suddenly I saw a clear image of Baba," he remembers, "stretching from the ground to the sky. Just as clear as if he was standing in front of me. Orange robe, moon-sized eyes, humongous afro. Then in the clouds around him, I saw images of Christ and other beings. I looked at the joint and said, 'I don't think I need this.' "

The huge image of Sai Baba in the sky lasted for about five minutes. After it faded, Michael went back inside the hotel room and tried to meditate. But when he closed his eyes, he saw a tiny, pinpoint image of Christ. With his eyes still closed, the image got bigger and brighter until it was so dazzling, so painfully bright that he had to open his eyes. For the next three days, Michael saw the image of Christ everywhere he looked, as if it had been burned into the retina of his mind.

"My whole attitude shifted from then on," Michael recalls. "I knew that my life would not be the same. I was a whole new person."

Today, Michael D. is a professional storyteller, living in Los Angeles. He's been drug-free for over ten years, and he left his life of sexual excess behind him long ago. Although he tells many kinds of stories, he specializes in tales of Africa and African Americans, delighting school children and people of all ages with his exuberant, joyful tellings. He is also an active member of the Sai Baba organization, and travels around the country sharing a different body of tales—the tales of how Sai Baba saved his life before he ever met him, and how the Indian holy man has guided him to a better, healthier life in body, mind, and spirit.

SEPTEMBER

Praise this world to the angel . . .

—RAINER MARIA RILKE,
DUINO ELEGIES

Angels and
Arrow Prayers

Wendy was twenty-one years old—smart, blonde, beautiful, and funny—full of promise for good things to come. She had just started taking classes in the dental hygiene program at Phoenix College. Always a straight-A student, Wendy had no problem with the science classes and she liked what dental hygiene had to offer: a well-paying job with time enough to have a life. That's what Wendy really wanted—a life.

She and her boyfriend Steve were driving home from a football game at Arizona State University. It was Friday night, September 13, 1975. As they approached her apartment complex, Wendy sat comfortably in the passenger seat, her left leg curled beneath her, her left arm reaching behind Steve in the driver's seat. Neither of them were wearing seatbelts. The last thing Wendy remembers is talking about what kind of pizza they would order when they got to her apartment.

Suddenly a glowing ball of light hurtled toward her out of the darkness, transforming the common reality of a Friday night date into a strange world of ethereal sounds and sights and feelings. Later Wendy discovered what had happened. A drunk driver had run a red light, smashing into their moving car at a combined impact of ninety miles per hour. Steve's car was knocked across the intersection, where it toppled a traffic signal and finally came to rest, crumpled from end to end like an accordion.

When the rescue crews arrived, they found Steve's head smashed into the windshield. Working frantically to pull him out of the wreckage, they assumed he was alone in the car and, unconscious, he was unable to tell them otherwise. But then a policeman walked around to the passenger side and shined his flashlight on the seat. He noticed a two-inch swatch of blonde hair sticking out from under the crumpled dashboard.

Now a new rescue effort began, with the workers torching through the metal to free Wendy. As they pulled her out of the car and laid her on the stretcher, it seemed to her as if she had entered a bizarre netherworld between life and death.

"I felt like I was slipping in and out of reality," she remembers today, "without any ability to will my conscious mind. I could hear voices, but all I remember were the urgent tones and quick movements around me. Now I was in a noisy ambulance, and the man's face above me was fuzzy, but visible. He was asking me stupid questions like, 'Do you know where you are?' Gee, and I was hoping *he* could tell *me*!"

The paramedic must have been administering CPR, because Wendy remembers trying to ask him "politely, but clearly" to get off her chest. It felt like a building on top of her! But when she opened her mouth to speak, she discovered that nothing would come out. She couldn't talk. Her brain seemed to be working—more or less—but she couldn't communicate with the world around her. By the time they arrived at the hospital, the reality of the situation was beginning to sink in. She was dying.

Now Wendy began to talk to herself, since she couldn't talk to anyone else. Soon her inner dialogue turned into prayers, what she calls "arrow prayers" today, because they were like arrows sent straight to God. Wendy had always felt as though she had a special friendship with God, but now she put that friendship to the test, asking Him to save her if it was possible. Even on the edge of death, she kept her sense of humor, throwing in an extra prayer that the doctor in the Hawaiian shirt wasn't drunk; she'd heard him mutter something about being at a party when he received the emergency page.

Whatever the condition of the doctor in the Hawaiian shirt, Wendy's condition took a turn for the worse. All of a sudden, she saw blood spurting out of a tube in her stomach, and she was on her way to the operating room. "I was beginning to feel cold and very weak," she remembers. "The center of my consciousness was floating inward; the people around me were less important and growing fainter. My monologue with God was my focus."

As they wheeled her into the operating room, Wendy's eyes were drawn toward something in the corner to her left. At first she thought it was someone praying in the traditional pose, with hands clasped and head bowed. But as she struggled to bring the image into focus, she realized that the "someone" didn't seem to be connected to the floor!

"It was a woman . . . soft and beautiful looking, and her face was like a kind of light that was extremely bright, but didn't hurt my eyes. And the more I focused on her, the more her face seemed to speak to me. It was like a telepathic communication, and she was telling me that I was going to be fine, and that I should have no fear. . . . Her presence flooded me with the most peaceful, relaxed emotion. I was completely resonant with this beautiful angel."

Wendy later discovered that her heart stopped twice during the operation because of low blood volume. She had a ruptured spleen, a severely damaged liver, a collapsed lung, and broken ribs. The surgeons used forty-two metal clips to put her body back together again.

After the surgery—and the vision of her angel—Wendy still hung between life and death. The turning point came four days later in the intensive care unit. She remembers floating above herself, seeing her body lying flat on the bed with monitors blinking and flashing behind. The floating Wendy felt free and light and good, not at all like the Wendy who lay in such terrible pain below. Suddenly the monitors began to scream, and the lines danced crazily across the screens. Four nurses and a doctor in a white coat converged around the bed, barking orders in a flurry of motion. Floating serenely above, Wendy watched the doctor insert a long needle into her body on the bed. But she noticed something else as well—a man in a brown coat, sitting to her left. His head was lowered, and he had intertwined the smallest finger of his own right hand with the smallest finger of Wendy's right hand, connecting them like an anchor to a boat.

In the midst of the medical crisis, Wendy heard the words, "You're going to make it." Then the man in the brown coat disappeared, along with the floating Wendy above the bed. "All at once I felt a heaviness and an excruciating pain in my chest," she recalls. "I was alive!"

In the following days, Wendy tried to find out more about the man in the brown coat. But no one knew anything about him. There was a Catholic priest at the hospital, but he wore a black cassock and he hadn't visited Wendy. Nor had her family requested a minister. Strangest of all, perhaps, was the chair where the man had seemed to be sitting beside the bed—there wasn't any chair on that side of the bed.

Wendy spent a month in the hospital, and it was almost a year before she recovered from her extensive injuries, learning to walk and move all over again. She missed her first year of dental hygiene school, but started again the following September. Today, twenty years later, Wendy works as a dental hygienist in southern California. She's married to a wonderful man, a man she believes is her soul mate, and she's a loving mother to their son. She's still smart, blonde, beautiful, and funny. But she carries something else beneath the surface—an inner light, an inner peace—a gift from the angels who came to her when she sent her arrow prayers to God.

THE WOUNDS OF
ST. FRANCIS

By the year 1224 Francis of Assisi had given up daily leadership of his order of friars and withdrawn to a life of solitude and contemplation. In September of that year, accompanied by three companions, he was on a forty-day retreat of fasting and prayer at La Verna, in the rugged Apennine Mountains of Italy.

Julien Green, a modern biographer of Francis, describes La Verna from personal experience: "One couldn't imagine a more wildly beautiful place. An Old Testament prophet couldn't have chosen a better refuge with a grandeur more dramatic or more favorable for dialogue with the Eternal."

... dialogue with the Eternal. Like all mystics, this was Francis's abiding passion. He wanted not only to worship Christ and teach His gospel, but also to experience union with Christ, or as Green puts it, "to share with Christ all the tortures of his passion." On the night of September 14, Francis got his wish.

While praying alone outside a cave, Francis was touched by a flaming angel carrying the image of Christ on the cross. We may consider this apparition to be a vision or a dream, but contemporary accounts indicate that it was something more. One of Francis's companions, Brother Leo, reported seeing a ball of fire descending from the heavens to Francis's face and then rising up again. And people who lived in the surrounding countryside saw the summit of La Verna illuminated as if by the rising sun.

Whatever the exact nature of the vision, all accounts agree that mysterious wounds opened on Francis's own hands and feet and side—similar to the wounds that afflicted Christ. When Francis and his companions descended from the mountain at the end of September, his hands and feet were wrapped in cloth, for he did not want to "advertise" the strange wounds. But the wound in his side drenched his tunic with blood, and his bandages had to be changed regularly. Francis bore these wounds for the rest of his life, and carried them with him into his grave when he died only two years later. During these two years, the wounds never healed and never showed signs of infection.

The experience of St. Francis was the first clearly-recorded case of the extraordinary phenomenon known as the stigmata. (There were several other vague reports around the same time, and in a first century epistle St. Paul wrote, "I bear the marks of Jesus branded on my body.") Although this event occurred over 750 years ago, in an age when visions and miracles were more readily accepted than they are today, there are many convincing contemporary accounts of Francis's stigmata. The clearest and most detailed description comes from his friend and biographer, Thomas of Celano, who indicated that Francis not only bore the wounds of Christ but also seemed to bear the nails as well:

> His hands and feet seemed pierced in the midst by nails, the heads of the nails appearing in the inner part of the hands and in the upper part of the feet . . . these marks were round on the inner side of the hands and elongated on the outer side, and certain small pieces of flesh were seen like the ends of nails bent and driven back, projecting from the rest of the flesh. So also the marks of the nails were imprinted in his feet and raised above the rest of the flesh. Moreover, his right side, as [if] it had been pierced by a lance, was overlaid with a scar, and often shed forth blood so that his tunic and drawers were many times sprinkled with the sacred blood.

If the stigmata of St. Francis were the beginning and end of the story, it would be no more than a curious footnote in medieval history. But the mystical experience of Francis apparently opened the door to a steady stream of stigmatic experiences that has continued unabated to the present day. A late nineteenth-century French physician, Dr. A. Imbert-Gourbeyre counted over three hundred recorded cases from the time of Francis to the publication of his own work in 1894, and stigmatists have continued to appear in the twentieth century.

The most famous modern stigmatists were the German ascetic Theresa Neumann, who died in 1962, and the Italian holy man, Padre Pio, who died in 1968. Pio belonged to the Capuchins—one of three orders that developed out of Francis's original order of friars—and like St. Francis, his stigmata also developed in September.

Padre Pio's wounds first appeared on September 7, 1910, less than a month after he was ordained as a priest. Although Pio was committed to being a "perfect victim," offering his own suffering to aid in the salvation of souls, he was embarrassed by this visible display and prayed that the stigmata be taken away. The wounds disappeared, only to return again on exactly the same day a year later. Once again the wounds disappeared. But this was only the beginning.

On the morning of September 20, 1918, after saying mass at the friary of San Giovanni Rotondo in southern Italy, Padre Pio had a terrifying vision of Christ. He was so frightened by the vision, in fact, that he later wrote that he felt he was going to die. But then: "The vision of the person faded away, and I noticed that my hands and feet and chest had been pierced and were bleeding profusely."

Padre Pio carried the stigmata to the end of his life—a period of fifty years—and during that time his wounds were carefully studied by physicians trained in modern medicine. A report by Dr. Luigi Romanelli, the chief of staff at a local hospital, confirms the physical reality of the inexplicable wounds:

Padre Pio has a very deep cut in the fifth intercostal space on the left side, seven or eight centimeters long, parallel to the ribs. The depth is great, but it is very difficult to ascertain. On his hand, there is an abundance of arterial blood. The borders of the wounds are not inflamed. . . . When I pressed with my fingers on the palm and back of his hand there was a sensation of empty space. . . . The lesions of the feet have the same characteristics as those of the hands. . . . I have examined Padre Pio five times in the course of fifteen months, and while I have sometimes noted some modifications in the lesions, I have never been able to classify them in any known clinical order.

A later examination by another Italian physician, Dr. Giorgio Festa, also confirmed the reality of the wounds and the fact that they passed right through his hand. ". . . I would have to answer and confirm under oath, so much is the certitude of the impression received, that I would be able to read something or to see an object if it were placed behind the hand."

A more recent case of stigmata began on September 13, 1972, when Clorette Robinson, a ten-year-old girl from Oakland, California, developed the wounds while attending school. The school nurse confirmed the fact that she was bleeding from her palms, although she could see no evidence of the wounds. Later, a pediatrician at the local hospital, Dr. Ella Collier, dressed the wounds in a "boxing-glove" type bandage, that completely surrounded her hand.

"There was no way she could undo that bandage or slip anything inside to make her hand bleed," Dr. Collier reported. "When I unwrapped it eighteen hours later, there was blood all over the inside of the bandage. I cleaned her hand. Then as I watched, blood began to appear again. It started in a small pool the size of a pea and spread over the palm."

Clorette's stigmata continued for about six months. Her case is especially interesting, not only for her youth and the fact that it occurred quite recently in a big American city, but also because she was a member of the Baptist

Church—one of the few non-Catholics to experience stigmata. Even more recently, an American priest named Father James Bruse apparently developed stigmata along with other miraculous powers in 1991.

Unlike many miracles, the scientific community does not question the existence of stigmata. But most scientific researchers see it as more of a ''hysterical'' illness than a truly supernatural occurrence. Nonetheless, there are many aspects of the phenomenon that are impossible to explain by natural causes—whether physical or psychological. This is especially true in a case like Padre Pio's, where the wounds were absolutely undeniable and continued for fifty years without showing normal signs of festering or inflammation. As his personal physician pointed out, Padre Pio lost a cup of blood every day for fifty years without showing signs of anemia.

Of course, for true believers the stigmata is more than a miraculous phenomenon; it is an affirmation of faith, a physical sharing of Christ's burden in saving the souls of the world.

Theresa Neumann's stigmata and other miraculous experiences are described in ''The Woman Who Didn't Eat'' in July, while the story of Father James Bruse is told in ''Tears, Blood, and Father Jim'' in November. Padre Pio also appears in ''The Mysterious Visitor,'' which follows this story, and ''The Pear Tree and the City of Roses'' in October.

THE MYSTERIOUS
VISITOR

St. Francis began his ministry after hearing voices in San Damiano, a run-down church located at the edge of Assisi. This story took place over 750 years later, in a small Italian village of the same name.

ROSA QUATTRINI HAD BEEN SICK FOR MOST OF HER adult life. All three of her children had been born by cesarean section, and the first birth left Rosa with a ventral hernia (a tear in the abdominal wall) that only seemed to get worse with each succeeding birth. Although doctors tried to repair the hernia when Rosa gave birth to her youngest child in 1952, they were apparently unsuccessful and Rosa's condition deteriorated. By 1958 she suffered from severe abdominal pain and intestinal blockage. She could barely eat, and was soon so weak that she had to stay in bed much of the time.

Three years later, Rosa's chronic condition turned acute, and she was hospitalized twice in 1961, first from March 6 to March 14, then again from June 30 to July 8. Hospital records indicate that Rosa suffered from severe abdominal pains accompanied by vomiting and loss of appetite, and that there was a large tear in her abdominal wall. Although it's unclear exactly what treatment Rosa received, she later reported that she was sent home with no hope of recovery, and within a few weeks of her release she was sicker than she had been before entering the hospital.

Then, just before noon on September 29, 1961, there was a knock on the door of Rosa's apartment in the northern Italian village of San Damiano. Rosa was in bed, cared for only by her Aunt Adele, who went to answer the door. She discovered a beautiful young woman with light-colored hair, dressed in a cheap bluish-gray dress and carrying a black purse. The young woman told Adele that she had come from very far away, and that she was collecting alms for Padre Pio—a well-known holy man who lived in the southern Italian friary of San Giovanni Rotondo. The young woman asked for a donation of 1,500 lire, a substantial amount of money for a poor family.

By this time, Padre Pio had already been credited with many miraculous cures, and Adele was aware of his work—though she was skeptical of his abilities. She told the young woman that while she had always contributed in the past, she could not contribute now. They only had 1,000 lire in the house, and even that was borrowed. When she mentioned that her niece was sick, the young woman asked to see her.

Adele led the visitor into the sick room, and the young woman asked Rosa what was wrong. Rosa said that she was "terribly wounded" and that she had been sent home from the hospital because there was no hope of recovering. Just as the words left Rosa's mouth, the noon bells rang at the local church, and the young woman told Rosa to rise from her bed. When Rosa said she could not, the young woman stretched out both her hands to help her. As she grasped the visitor's hands, Rosa felt a jolt of energy and found herself able to get up from the bed, shouting, "I am healed! I am healed!"

The young woman told Rosa to say certain prayers according to the instructions of Padre Pio, and after she finished the prayers the mysterious visitor placed her hands over Rosa's abdomen and healed the wounds. According to one story, the woman also made a special mixture of water, earth, olive leaf, and a consecrated candle and told Rosa to drink a little of the mixture for the next three days at five o'clock each morning—the time when Padre Pio said Mass. She then told Rosa to visit Padre Pio as soon as possible, and assured her that the money for the trip would come to her.

Although Rosa's Aunt Adele was skeptical of Padre Pio's healing powers, she gave the young visitor five hundred lire in thanks for the grace that had apparently touched her sick niece. The young woman then left the way she had come, but out of a group of children playing in the street, only Rosa's youngest son saw her pass.

Once the visitor was gone, Adele wondered aloud whether she had been right to give her the five hundred lire—half the money they had in the house. After all, they didn't even know who she was or if she was actually collecting alms for Padre Pio. But Rosa assured her that she really did feel much better. Adele then went into her own room, where she had a statue of Mary, and prayed that the money would go to Padre Pio. Suddenly she heard a strong, clear voice saying, "Have confidence, your sick one will be healed."

And indeed, after over twenty years of chronic illness, Rosa Quattrini was apparently healed by the mysterious visit. She began to take an active part in the life of her local parish, and the following May she joined a group of pilgrims who went to visit Padre Pio in southern Italy. Just as the visitor had predicted, the money to finance Rosa's trip arrived from an unknown source.

In San Giovanni Rotondo, while sitting in the square outside Padre Pio's church, Rosa saw the mysterious young woman again. By this time, Rosa had come to believe that her visitor was really Mary, the Madonna. She mentioned her belief to the young woman, who replied that she was "the Mother of Consolation and the Afflicted." Although Rosa was sitting with another pilgrim from her home parish during this conversation, her companion saw nothing.

The next morning, after attending Mass in Padre Pio's church, the young woman appeared beside Rosa near the altar and led her into the sacristy, where Padre Pio was waiting. When Rosa explained that she was confused by the events of the previous months, Padre Pio pointed to the young woman standing beside them and said, "There is the one who will confirm it for you." He then told Rosa to go home and take care of the sick.

For the next two years, Rosa Quattrini devoted herself to caring for the sick in her home region. Although she had no formal training, she apparently had unusual success with several difficult patients. Throughout this period, Rosa always felt that she was being guided by Padre Pio, and on one occasion the holy man even appeared to her and told her to go to a particular hospice where she would find "another soul to care for and to save." When Rosa arrived at the hospice, she discovered that the mother superior was indeed looking for someone to care for a particularly difficult patient, but she had not yet spoken to anyone about it.

In September 1964, Rosa made a second pilgrimage to visit Padre Pio, who said that her healing mission was over and that she should return home where a great event awaited her. A month later, on October 16, 1964, the great event occurred and Rosa Quattrini began a new phase in her miraculous life.

For the rest of Rosa's story, see "The Pear Tree and the City of Roses" in October.

MAYBE A MAN
ON HORSEBACK

IN THE FALL OF 1976, GUY MOUNT WAS RESEARCHING the medicinal herbs used by southern California Indians during childbirth. The research was part of Mount's work as a graduate student in anthropology, but it also had a deep personal significance. Mount had helped his wife deliver their own children at home, and he believed that the Indians had much to teach the white world about natural healing methods.

One of Mount's primary sources of information was an elderly Serrano Indian woman named Magdalina Nombre. After she told him of her own experiences with natural childbirth, she suggested that he go and talk with her niece, Ruby Modesto, who belonged to the neighboring Cahuilla tribe. "She knows all about plants and everything," said Magdalina.

Mount was eager to talk with Ruby, but the directions he received for finding her house were so vague that he almost gave up the idea of the journey. "I was told she lived in the desert near Martinez Reservation," he later explained, "and that I should drive toward that location, turn left at Valerie Jean's Date Shop, and 'maybe' a man on horseback would tell me where to find Ruby. I sincerely thought driving south into the intense heat of Coachella Valley and looking for a man on horseback was a wild-goose chase. But my thoughts were a worthless barrier to discovery. . . ."

Most people prepare for a journey by packing the material goods they might need. Mount took a different approach—unpacking the doubts that stood in his way. "I had to clear my mind through meditation, and trust that I would be guided on a path that was mysterious in nature."

As a graduate student on a shoestring budget, Mount also had to deal with a more material mystery: coming up with twenty bucks to fill the gas tank of his VW van and have some change in his pocket. A week later, when his mind was clear and his gas tank was full, Guy Mount left the University of Riverside and drove out into the desert, past Palm Springs to the city of Indio. It was about one hundred degrees in Indio, and Mount knew it would get hotter as he continued on into the Coachella Valley. He'd never been past Indio, and he'd never heard of Valerie Jean's Date Shop. "It was all pretty obscure," he says today. But he had resolved to follow the path he had been given without question.

As he drove south into the desert, dipping below sea level, the temperature reached one hundred twenty degrees. Finally he reached the Martinez Reservation and turned left at Valerie Jean's Date Shop. There, in the middle of a paved road, he immediately encountered a man on horseback—who cheerfully pointed the way to the Modesto house. Mount found Ruby and her husband, David, sitting under the shade of their ramada, as if they were waiting for him.

The meeting with Ruby Modesto was a turning point in the life of Guy Mount. For Ruby not only knew all about medicinal plants, she carried within her a deep, living knowledge of the spiritual beliefs and practices of the Cahuilla people. Mount discovered that Ruby Modesto was a *pul*, a traditional Cahuilla shamaness who had power to heal souls and perform other works of wonder. As their relationship deepened, Ruby agreed to collaborate with him on the story of her own life and the spiritual practices of her people.

The book was published in 1980, just a few months after Ruby's death. Entitled *Not for Innocent Ears: Spiritual*

Traditions of a Desert Cahuilla Medicine Woman, it provides a lasting record of an extraordinary way of life that is rapidly fading into the past. For Guy Mount, it was also the beginning of a new life as the owner and publisher of Sweetlight Books, a small press dedicated to books about American Indians and other subjects that reflect his deep love and respect for the earth.

It's strange how small miracles can change our lives. For Guy Mount, the change came when he decided to cast his doubts away and believe that a man on horseback would show him the way.

OCTOBER

And if you would know God be not
therefore a solver of riddles.
Rather look about you and you shall see
Him playing with your children.
And look into space; you shall see Him
walking in the cloud, outstretching His arms
in the lightning and descending in rain.
You shall see Him smiling in flowers,
then rising and waving His hands in trees.

—KAHLIL GIBRAN, *THE PROPHET*

THE PEAR TREE AND
THE CITY OF ROSES

After over twenty years of chronic illness, a poor Italian woman named Rosa Quattrini was healed by a young woman who appeared at her door, collecting alms for the holy man Padre Pio. The story of Rosa's healing is told in "The Mysterious Visitor" in September. Here's the rest of Rosa's story.

IN OCTOBER 1964, ROSA QUATTRINI HAD RECENTLY RE-turned from her second visit to the Italian holy man Padre Pio, who had predicted that a great event awaited her. Around 11:30 on the morning of October 16, a neighbor stopped by to ask a favor of Rosa, something no one would have done three years earlier, when Rosa was a bedridden invalid unable to even care for herself. But much had happened since then, and Rosa Quattrini was now a healthy and active member of her community.

Rosa and the neighbor chatted for awhile, and the neighbor left just as the noon bells began to ring in the local church. As she listened to the bells, Rosa recited the Angelus—a prayer that pious Catholics recite along with the bells. The Angelus had special meaning for Rosa, because it was during the ringing of the noon bells that she had been cured of her long, painful illness—cured by the touch of a mysterious young woman she believed to be the Virgin Mary.

Now, in the middle of her prayer, Rosa heard a woman's voice calling to her. "Come, come, I am waiting for you!" Rosa left her house and went out into a nearby vineyard, where she saw a dazzling light. As Rosa approached, the light became brighter and the voice grew sweeter and more powerful, calling for her to come. Rosa walked farther into the vineyard, sat down on a footstool, and made the sign of the cross with her rosary. Suddenly, a cloud descended from the sky, with gold and silver stars dancing around it and roses showering down but never reaching the ground.

The cloud settled over a plum tree, and a red globe of light appeared on the branches of a nearby pear tree. In an instant, the cloud over the plum tree disappeared and Rosa saw Mary in all her glory—no longer the poor young woman who had come to her door in cheap clothing, but rather the Queen of Heaven. She wore a white cloak and a blue gown, tied at the waist with a white sash. From the sash hung a rosary with a living figure of Christ on the crucifix. A necklace of stars adorned her neck, and rays of light shot out from the open palms of her hands.

Rosa fell to her knees and told Mary that she was not worthy to see her in such dazzling glory, but that she would listen to whatever she had to say. Looking beautiful but sad, Mary crossed from the plum tree to the pear tree, where the globe of red light still hovered. "Listen, my daughter," she said, "I have come from afar to announce to the world that it is necessary to pray, to pray much, for Jesus can no longer carry the cross. You must help him carry it."

When Mary told Rosa to deliver the message to her parish priest, Rosa replied that she was afraid people would take her for a fool. She asked for some sign so that others would believe her, and Mary promised to make the trees flower. Then she began to rise from the pear tree, smiling at Rosa as rose petals fell from her hands. Rosa watched in amazement as Mary continued to rise higher and higher, floating off toward the local church, until she finally disappeared.

When Rosa looked back at the pear tree—which had

been bare of flowers a few moments earlier—she saw that it had erupted in the full bloom of spring, just as Mary had promised. The branch of the plum tree where Mary had first appeared also burst with flowers. All the other branches and all the surrounding trees bore the usual appearance of mid-October foliage in north-central Italy.

News of the miraculous apparition spread quickly through the small community; among the first to hear were the Italian and American flyers at a base located near the Quattrini home. That afternoon, a group of these flyers, including an American general, were apparently among the first to join Rosa in praying at the base of the pear tree. Two days later, a crowd of local people gathered to pray at the tree, and many of them remember very clearly that the pear tree was completely white with the blossoms of spring although it was mid-fall and summer fruit still hung on its branches.

The miraculous blossoms lasted for almost three weeks, despite heavy rains, and at first it was the strange sight of the blossoming pear tree that attracted people to San Damiano. But Rosa claimed that Mary appeared to her many more times; in fact, according to some stories Mary appeared to Rosa regularly every Friday. Soon pilgrims began to arrive from Italy and other European countries to see the site of the miraculous apparitions and to hear Rosa's messages from the Madonna.

During several appearances in 1965 and 1966, Mary instructed Rosa to have a well dug at a particular spot where she would find a pure, healing water that would cleanse both body and soul. The well was dug on the spot, and though there were difficulties in the digging process, Rosa always seemed to know in advance about the specific layers of rock the diggers would encounter. Finally, in 1967, the well was completed when a vein of water was found at a depth of seventeen meters, exactly as Rosa had predicted.

Around the same time, the Madonna ordered Rosa to build a "City of Roses" on the site where she had appeared. The City would be devoted to good works, with charitable institutions for the care of orphans, the elderly, and the sick. Various organizations were formed to finance this project, and a good beginning was made, with Rosa's supporters buying specific pieces of land and houses on Rosa's instructions.

By 1965, Rosa Quattrini's efforts at San Damiano became complicated by the internal politics of the Catholic Church, which was going through a period of upheaval following the changes instituted by the Second Vatican Council. The Church was skeptical about Rosa's story, and over the years, various church officials issued statements denying the authenticity of the apparitions, even going so far as to order Rosa to stop speaking publicly about her experiences. Some of this official skepticism was due to the situation itself, since the truth of the apparitions depended primarily on the reports of a single witness—Rosa Quattrini—although many other people testified to the blossoming pear tree and Rosa's earlier healing.

However, it's also clear that the Church's skepticism stems from the fact that some of Rosa's strongest supporters were followers of the conservative French bishop, Marcel Lefebvre, who led a vocal and open resistance to the Church's new liberal policies. Rosa herself wanted no part in this conflict, and it says something of her loyalty to the Church that upon her death in September 1981, she left all the assets of her City of Roses project to the pope. It also says something of the pope's attitude that he refused Rosa's bequest.

At the time of her death, an Italian district attorney had frozen Rosa's assets and was conducting a criminal investigation into possible fraud regarding the City of Roses project. However, the charges of fraud were dismissed in 1982, when a magistrate found no evidence of any wrongdoing in fund-raising for the City of Roses. Moreover, neither Rosa while she was alive nor her family after her death, used the money for their personal gain. The houses that had been purchased in Rosa's name were used as hotels for pilgrims who came to the site of the San Damiano apparitions, and the charges for their lodging were extremely reasonable.

Around the same time that the charges of fraud were dismissed, a new organization took over administration of the City of Roses project. By 1988, the organization was administering two houses for pilgrims, a home for the elderly, an infirmary, and a youth center. This new organization has apparently made its peace with the Catholic Church, and its literature de-emphasizes the role of Rosa Quattrini and the cult that grew around her after she reported the appearance of the Virgin Mary.

The story of Rosa Quattrini is one of the most complex, controversial, and intriguing tales of miraculous apparitions in the modern age. Although many questions remain—and are unlikely to be answered—several truly miraculous aspects of the story seem quite clear.

Rosa Quattrini did regain her health in September 1961, around the time she claimed to have received a visit from a mysterious young woman collecting alms for Padre Pio. Rosa's sudden change in health was attested by many people in the community, and though her hospital records from early 1961 indicated a severe tear in her abdominal wall from her cesarean sections, two doctors and a nurse who saw her during a later, unrelated illness in 1970 all indicated that the scars from her cesarean sections were completely healed with no evidence of a tear.

And though we have only Rosa's word regarding the apparitions of the Madonna, a pear tree in the vineyard near Rosa's house did erupt in the full bloom of spring on October 16, 1964. Hundreds of people saw this tree, and the story was covered in several local newspapers.

But perhaps the most miraculous aspect of Rosa's story is this: a poor sick woman who could barely leave her bed completely turned her life around and—despite official opposition—founded a genuine, well-meaning charitable organization called the City of Roses.

I Had a Dream
Last Night

Rosalie was raised in the Chicago area during the '50s and early '60s—the early wave of the Baby Boomer generation born after World War II. But Rosalie had a different and more difficult childhood than most Boomers. Her parents were both European Jews who had survived the Holocaust. They arrived in America scarred and broken, and found little help in coping with their pain. As Rosalie points out, "Today we have counseling for the survivors of plane crashes, but the survivors of the Holocaust didn't have any counseling."

Rosalie's mother suffered from severe depression, and spent most of Rosalie's childhood in bed, too drugged with a combination of antidepressants to function as a normal parent. Rosalie's father wasn't much of a parent, either. Orphaned at the age of eight, he had been raised in a Jewish school called a Yeshiva, where he studied the Torah but never learned to be part of a functioning family. When the war began, he ran away from the Yeshiva, only to be imprisoned in a concentration camp. He just didn't know how to be a father.

With such emotionally-wounded parents, Rosalie grew up feeling as if she were the parent and they were the children. "They never took care of me," she says today. "I always took care of them."

At the age of seventeen, Rosalie left home and went to

Israel, where she met a handsome, intelligent Israeli named Shai. It was love at first sight, and they married the following year—the same year that Shai fought in the Six Day War. Two children soon followed, and Shai went away again to fight in the Yom Kippur War. Then a third baby. From a childhood taking care of her parents, Rosalie was quickly thrust into an adulthood taking care of her children.

In the late '70s, Shai and Rosalie moved to the United States, where Shai had been offered a doctoral fellowship to study history at the University of Chicago. For Rosalie it was a bittersweet return to her hometown after a decade in Israel.

The years passed and the children grew. Shai earned a Ph.D. in Middle Eastern History and established an insurance practice, while Rosalie ran a business of her own. Like many couples, their marriage had its ups and downs, but there was something deeper, simmering dangerously beneath the surface. Every six or seven years, their marriage erupted in crisis, spewing forth hot anger and ill feeling so intense that it threatened the survival of their union. Each time Shai and Rosalie managed to work out their differences, and their relationship would continue, stronger than before—until the next crisis.

In 1986, after almost twenty years of marriage, they faced their third and most difficult marital crisis. During a long car trip to Canada, they finally became so beaten and exhausted by their ongoing conflict that they just couldn't fight anymore. So they stopped. They withdrew from the battlefield. And with a strange sense of wonder, Shai and Rosalie realized that this was the beginning of an answer, like a light waiting at the end of a long, dark tunnel. To save their marriage, they needed to "surrender" to each other, to give in with unconditional love. But realizing it was easier than doing it, especially for Rosalie.

"I was in a tremendous amount of emotional pain," she recalls. "We were having a difficult time with our relationship, and I was feeling very helpless. I kept having strange dreams night after night, as well as nightmares, but could not get to the essence of my emotional pain. I felt that I had one of my life's greatest problems to solve, but I had no strength left to solve it.''

The dreams and nightmares continued for years, with Rosalie struggling to understand the meaning behind her pain. What was wrong? Why was she unable to surrender to her husband, to give him unconditional love? Shai did his best. He tried to surrender in his own way, to give her the love that she withheld. And he seemed to know whenever she was having a nightmare. He would wake her and save her from the terror—for the moment. But the struggle continued.

Then in the early morning of October 2, 1992, Rosalie finally touched the light at the end of the tunnel. It was the time between Rosh Hashanah and Yom Kippur, the one time of the year when Jewish people believe that the heavens are open and human life is being reviewed by God. That morning, Rosalie had an extremely vivid dream. Not a nightmare, but a dream with echoes of pain.

''I was in a supermarket,'' she later wrote in her journal, ''and a little blonde girl was there with her mother. I felt the need to help her because her mother was incapable. . . . This little girl was myself, my past. It has always been difficult for me to connect this neglected child with the adult me.''

On the surface the dream was very simple, but for Rosalie the message was clear. Because of her difficult childhood, she had never learned to let go and trust. She had to maintain control, because she had grown up believing that the world would fall apart if she didn't. She was always giving to others, working to be a good friend, a good daughter, a good mother, a good wife. But it was also necessary to let others take care of her, to let others be good to her. Until she allowed that, she could never enjoy unconditional love with Shai, or with anyone else.

When she woke from the dream, Rosalie lay quietly, thinking about what she had just learned. It seemed extremely profound to her, as if it were the missing link in her emotional life. But how could she communicate it to Shai, sleeping soundly beside her? How could she say, ''I need to be taken care of; I need to let you take care of me"? It's difficult to expose oneself emotionally after a lifetime of hiding feelings and playing the role of the strong one.

Suddenly Shai opened his eyes and looked at Rosalie. "Come here," he said, reaching out to her and holding her in his arms. "I had a dream last night . . ." As Rosalie listened in wonder, Shai related the same dream. He had seen her as a little girl in a supermarket with her mother, a little girl who needed help because her mother was incapable. Without Rosalie having to say a word, he understood precisely what she was feeling. "Don't worry," he assured her lovingly, "I'm going to take care of you."

"We felt as if we crossed over to some mysterious realm," Rosalie explains today. "Our souls seemed to have melted into one another . . . and our relationship was saved from another terrible crisis. We both believe that event was a miracle and have felt a sacredness in our relationship since then."

THE TWO
RESURRECTIONS OF
JOHN SLOCUM

In the fall of 1881, John Slocum was logging the forests near Puget Sound. Slocum was a member of the Squaxin band, part of the Salish Indian group of the Pacific Northwest. Physically, he was a very ordinary man: about five feet eight inches, soft-spoken, stoop-shouldered, with a head that had been flattened at birth—a traditional practice of his people. Like many Indians in the area, he smoked, drank a little, and gambled too much. He was especially fond of betting on Indian pony races.

But that day, something extraordinary happened to this "ordinary" man. John Slocum broke his neck in a logging accident and was carried back to his house, where his family washed and dressed his body for burial and covered him with a white sheet. While his wife, Mary, and the rest of the family wailed in mourning, John's two half-brothers set out in a canoe to buy a coffin in the nearby town of Olympia.

They never needed the coffin. After a few hours, John began to move beneath the sheet. As the mourners watched with wonder and fear, he pulled the sheet away from his face, turned his head from side to side, stretched his arms, and sat up. Walking outside, he took off his clothes, washed with clean water, and wrapped himself in a clean sheet. He ordered Mary to throw away his burial clothes and the old sheet because they were things of his death.

When he came back inside, John asked everyone in the room to shake hands with him. Then he asked them to kneel with him and he began to pray. He announced that he had died and gone to the gates of heaven—the Christian heaven—where he met an angel who sent him back to earth with a message for the Indians:

They must stop smoking, drinking, gambling, and practicing Indian shamanism. They must pray and cross themselves every morning and evening and before meals. They must attend regular church services and build a church for John to preach in and continue his teachings. If they did these things, God would give them a great "medicine" to help them.

Ten years later, John Slocum described his heavenly experience through an interpreter:

> All at once I saw a shining light—great light—trying my soul. I looked and saw my body had no soul—looked at my own body—it was dead. . . . When I saw it, it was pretty poor. My soul left body and went up to judgment place of God. . . .
>
> I have seen a great light in my soul from that good land; I have understood all Christ wants us to do. Before I came alive I saw I was sinner. Angel in heaven said to me, "You must go back and turn alive again on earth."
>
> . . . When I came alive, I tell my friends, "Good thing in heaven. God is kind to us. If you all try hard and help me we will be better men on earth." And now we all feel that it is so.

John's family and neighbors built him a church, but on the appointed day the roof was not finished, so they stretched a tarp across the open space and John began to preach. Although Slocum's message was not that different from the teachings of the white missionaries, the fact that a local Indian had a direct experience in the Christian heaven stirred great excitement in the Puget Sound area, making a strong impression on people who were searching for their own religious identity. Ironically, the white missionaries—who had been trying to teach the Indians the same basic ideas that John Slocum espoused—rejected Slocum's ministry as being either imaginary or diabolic.

After a few months, the initial excitement over John Slocum's revelations faded, and Slocum himself seemed to forget his own teachings, sliding back to his old ways—especially his fondness for gambling. Then in 1882, about a year after his first experience, John Slocum almost died again. This time the cause was apparently sickness, but his father believed the real problem was an evil Indian "doctor" or shaman, and he insisted on hiring another Indian shaman to try and save his son.

John Slocum had preached against shamans, and his wife Mary was one of his strongest disciples. Even when John forgot his own teachings, Mary continued to follow them. Now, upset that her husband was under the power of a shaman, she ran in hysterics down to a creek near their house and began to wash her face. Suddenly she collapsed and her family and friends carried her back to the house.

When she regained consciousness, Mary moaned and trembled. Her hands shook uncontrollably, and the shaking soon spread throughout her body. She demanded that John be removed from the shaman's hut and brought into the house. The onlookers were so disturbed by Mary's strange appearance that they obeyed her and laid John's body in the center of the room, with blood pouring from his nose.

Mary ordered some of her relatives to stand in various positions around him, holding candles in their hands and extending their arms over his body. She handed her brother, Henry, a bell that John had used in his services and told him to ring it. Soon Henry was twitching and shaking just like Mary. Then the other two women in the room, Mary's mother and sister-in-law, caught "the shake" as well.

"He is going to live!" Mary cried in a loud, sobbing voice. "He is going to live!"

Suddenly, John Slocum's nose stopped bleeding, and he recovered miraculously from his near-fatal illness. At first he was suspicious of the shaking, because he thought it might be from the devil. But in time he decided that shaking was the powerful "medicine" that the angel had promised him in his original vision.

With the introduction of shaking, the Puget Sound religious movement gained new momentum. John Slocum was a simple, humble man and did not have the personality to lead a growing religious movement, so another Salish Indian named Louis Yowaluch took over leadership of the church—although Slocum was always honored for his original vision. For ten years, white missionaries and government agents persecuted Slocum, Yowaluch and the other Shaker leaders until finally, in 1892 the Shakers organized as a legal church under the Dawes Severalty Act, a new law that gave American Indians the same rights and privileges as other U.S. citizens, including the freedom to worship God in any way they choose.

Today the Indian Shaker Church is still a thriving religious organization in the Pacific Northwest. The Shakers have been credited with countless miraculous cures, as well as other wonders such as prophecies and finding lost objects. And it all began with the two resurrections of John Slocum.

VIRTUALLY
IMPOSSIBLE

In the foreword, I told the story of my parents' struggle to have a child. Almost forty years later, my wife and I faced a similar struggle, and though we never saw any visions, I believe we, too, were blessed by a miracle.

IN EARLY 1991, MARLENE AND I DECIDED TO HAVE A second child. Our son, Devin, was almost two and a half, and we wanted our children to be close enough in age to grow up together and play together as friends. Then too, we had to consider our own ages. We were already older parents—I was thirty-seven and Marlene was thirty-four—and Devin managed to wear us out all by himself. We didn't want to be too old for a second child.

Actually we had *decided* to have a second child the year before, but we had to wait for the pregnancy to be covered under our new health insurance, because we just weren't in a financial position to pay for it ourselves. At the time, the waiting period didn't seem like a big deal. Marlene had gotten pregnant immediately with Devin, so we assumed it would be easy again. But it wasn't. We tried month after month without success. As the months turned into a year, we began to get nervous.

Marlene discussed the problem with her obstetrician-gynecologist, Dr. Michael Price. He treated her with a fertility drug and ordered a series of tests, but the drug had no effect and the test results were negative. As far as he could tell, there was no reason why Marlene should be unable to conceive. He suggested that I have a sperm test.

Believe me, a sperm test is a strange experience for a man—and I'll skip the details. But stranger still were the results of the test. In late November 1991, Marlene and I sat in Dr. Price's office while he scanned the lab report. We've always been impressed by Dr. Price. He combines the two most important qualities of a physician: scientific intelligence and human compassion. He's also very honest.

"Based on these results," he said, "I'm afraid that it's virtually impossible for the two of you to conceive without some sort of intervention." He went on to explain the various options for intervention. They were expensive, and they wouldn't be covered by insurance. But it wasn't the money that bothered me. It was the strangeness of it all— the idea that a technician in a fertility laboratory was going to spin my sperm in a centrifuge and inject it into my wife. It seemed so cold and impersonal. So non-human.

Marlene didn't feel that way at all. She desperately wanted a second child and she saw the intervention as the only way to have that child. She wanted to begin the procedures immediately, but I resisted, asking for a little time to think it over. The next two months were among the rockiest we had ever experienced in our marriage. Marlene felt that I was being selfish, placing my own feelings ahead of her deep desire to have another child. And I suppose that was true. But I couldn't help believing that it would work out. If it had happened so naturally and easily with Devin, why wouldn't it happen again? What had changed?

What had changed, I realized, was my brain. In 1988, a few weeks after Marlene told me she was pregnant with our first child, I had a series of epileptic seizures. It had taken months before the seizures were fully controlled with medication, and during much of that time I was either confused by seizure activity or so drugged that I could barely function. Now, three years later, Tegretol—the medication that controlled my seizures—was such an integral part of my life that I didn't even think about it at first. But when I read the pharmaceutical information sheet, I discovered that Tegretol had been shown to stop sperm production in rats. I've never considered myself a rat, but it seemed like an interesting connection, so I called my neurologist, Dr. Michael Shack.

Dr. Shack had taken over my case a couple of years earlier, and I have enormous respect for his judgment. I was frankly disappointed when he told me that the results in laboratory rats had only been produced by massive doses, and he was absolutely positive that there was no such mechanism working in my case. He also assured me that if we did manage to conceive, the Tegretol would have no effect on the baby. But he suggested that I try getting off medication anyway. I had been on it now for four years, and with no underlying organic problem, he wasn't convinced that I needed a lifetime of medication.

The prospect of getting off medication was both exciting and frightening. On the one hand, nothing would make me happier than to stop taking this medication that made me so tired I had to sleep ten to twelve hours a night and drink endless cups of coffee during the day. On the other hand, how could I ever be sure that I wouldn't have another seizure? Of course the answer was that I couldn't be sure. But I decided it was worth the chance.

In the meantime, Marlene and I began to pray more than we had ever prayed during our marriage. Marlene was raised Jewish, while I was raised Catholic. But I left the Church when I was fifteen years old, and though Marlene usually attends synagogue on High Holy Days, she has never been a traditionally religious Jew. Now we began to reach toward God with a new sincerity, asking that He help us have another child. We even asked our friends to pray for us in our annual holiday letter.

My friends prayed in their way, and Marlene prayed in hers. I won't speak for them. But the most difficult aspect of my own prayers was trying to imagine God. When I had prayed as a Catholic child, the images were easy: God was an old man with a long white beard; Jesus a young man with a dark beard; the Holy Spirit a white dove; and the Virgin Mary a beautiful lady in a blue dress. But now I found myself thinking that maybe God doesn't have a face at all. Maybe God is a power, an essence, the soul of the universe. So I prayed to that power, that essence, that soul. And there were moments, deep in the middle of the night, when I knew—as surely as I know my name—that God was listening.

In January 1992, I went to see a urologist named Sanford Behrens. For me, this was a last attempt to find a scientific answer before beginning the intervention procedures at the fertility clinic. Again I encountered a fine physician who discussed the issues with intelligence and compassion. During a second visit, on January 29, Dr. Behrens and I actually looked at my sperm sample under a microscope and he showed me exactly what was wrong. There just weren't enough active cells to facilitate pregnancy. Although he hesitated to say it was "impossible," Dr. Behrens told me that it was "highly unlikely" that we would be able to conceive naturally. By this time, I had been off Tegretol for a few days, but Dr. Behrens agreed that the medication should have no effect on my sperm production, and he pointed out that even if there was some effect, it would take about three months before new sperm could be produced.

After my visit with Dr. Behrens I decided to go forward with the intervention. Marlene was very happy, but her home tests indicated that she would ovulate on the second Sunday in February—and the fertility clinic wasn't open on Sunday! So we decided to wait until March. Now that I had made the leap and agreed to go forward, Marlene felt more relaxed about the issue and suddenly a month didn't seem like such a long time to wait.

On Monday, February 10, 1992, Marlene got pregnant—naturally, the way God created men and women to make children. We know the exact date because she felt such terrible pain that day that we went to see Dr. Price. He said she was ovulating, though he was unable to explain why it caused such pain. I'm unable to explain it either. Nor am

I able to explain how Marlene got pregnant twelve days after an extremely competent physician showed me—under a microscope—why it wouldn't happen. Or why she got pregnant less than three months after another extremely competent physician told us it was "virtually impossible." I cannot explain it, that is, except by calling it a miracle.

Of course, our real miracle arrived nine months later, on October 30, 1992, when Marlene gave birth to a beautiful baby girl, Dariel Anne Walker. That also happens to be Marlene's birthday, which seemed fitting to me, for this was the child that Marlene wanted so desperately, the answer to her prayers—and to my prayers to a God I struggled to imagine.

Today Dariel is a delightful little girl who looks a lot like Marlene except that her eyes are mine. Every time I hold her in my arms, I think of the miraculous power that is there for those who ask with a sincere heart. And I often think of another miracle that came to me along with my precious daughter. For in trying to find a way to bring her into the world, I stopped taking seizure medication. It's been three years now, and I feel as if I'm a new person—clear-headed and full of energy. My writing career has taken off in a way that would have been impossible while I was still on medication. And though I'm still an "old parent," I do a pretty good job of keeping up with my two young children.

Despite what the doctors told me, I still wonder if the medication had some effect on our ability to have a second child. But whether it did or whether it didn't, I know this for sure: with God's help—no matter how we imagine God—nothing is "virtually impossible."

NOVEMBER

When in fortunate hours we ponder this miracle, the wise man doubts if at all other times he is not blind and deaf; for the universe becomes transparent, and the light of higher laws than its own shines through it.

—RALPH WALDO EMERSON, *NATURE*

SLAIN IN THE SPIRIT

When I first corresponded with Paulette DeMauro, she wrote, "My life has been full of one miracle after another." Although the following story describes only a few of those miracles, I think you'll agree.

IN 1975, PAULETTE DEMAURO DRESSED HERSELF UP AS a baby doll for Halloween. It seemed appropriate, for she had an eleven-month-old "baby doll" of her own, a sweet little girl named Jennifer. The truth is, Paulette was practically a baby herself, just twenty-one years old.

That night, when she went to wash the red rouge from her cheeks, the makeup wouldn't come off. Or at least that's how it seemed to Paulette at the time. She tried again the next morning, but her face was still red and splotchy. At first she thought it was some sort of strange reaction to the makeup, but as the days passed, rashes appeared on her arms and legs and she felt so tired she could barely move. Finally, in mid-November, Paulette went to see her physician, an old "country doctor" who practiced in a small town near Rochester, New York. After examining her and listening to her symptoms, he told her that she probably had lupus—either that or leukemia.

As it turned out, the doctor was surprisingly perceptive, for lupus was not as well known at that time as it is today. An inflammatory disease of the connective tissues, it can attack many different areas of the body, almost as if the

body were allergic to itself. Symptoms range from skin
rashes and joint pains to inflammation of the heart, lungs,
and other organs. The cause of the disease is unknown, and
though there are several courses of treatment, there is no
known cure.

The doctor sent her straight to the nearest hospital emergency room, but Paulette decided to wait until after the first
of the year before being hospitalized for further tests. She
had so much to do, with her daughter's first birthday and
the Christmas holidays. In early 1976, she had the necessary blood tests and saw a specialist in internal medicine.
The specialist confirmed that the condition was indeed sys-
temic lupus erythematosus, often called SLE. But then he
told Paulette and her mother something else, something
much more horrible and frightening. He said that Paulette
had six months to live.

Today, this seems like an extreme, almost hysterical
statement. Lupus can be fatal, but such cases are rare and
most people live fairly normal lives through an aggressive,
comprehensive treatment program. Twenty years ago, however, the prognosis for lupus was not as clear, and the doctor made this bleak statement in good faith. "It was like I
got hit in the face with a brick," Paulette recalls. "My
whole body went into shock. I remember going numb from
head to toe." At the age of twenty-one, with a one-year-
old baby girl, an apparently competent medical specialist
was telling her that she wouldn't live to see her daughter's
second birthday.

Paulette herself was an adopted, only child, and she
didn't want to put her parents through the pain of watching
her die. So when her husband was offered a job in Florida,
they decided to move south—not a wise move, in retrospect, because lupus causes extreme sensitivity to the sun.
Drained of energy and unable to go out into the glaring
Florida sun, Paulette spent much of her time watching TV
and soon found herself drawn into the strangely seductive
world of television evangelists. "I laugh now," she says
today of her fascination with the televangelists, "because
I've come so far since then. But it was a beginning." Al-

though she'd been raised a Catholic, the spiritual side of the Catholic Church never really worked for her. Now, facing the imminent reality of death, Paulette became born again as a Christian through the preachers on her television screen.

Six months passed and Paulette was alive, though she suffered from constant pain in her joints and overwhelming exhaustion. After almost a year in Florida, she and her family returned to the Rochester area. Her husband was out of work, and times were tough, but at least she was alive. Then Paulette became pregnant again. Ironically, she had been told the lupus would make it extremely difficult to get pregnant, so she had not been as careful as she might have been.

The steroid medications that Paulette took to control her lupus were very dangerous for a baby in the womb, and she was warned that the child would suffer multiple developmental problems, including physical deformities. "When do you want to make an appointment to terminate the pregnancy?" asked her obstetrician-gynecologist. Paulette replied that she didn't want to terminate it. Although she hadn't planned on getting pregnant, she believed that everything happens for a reason, and her own experience as an adopted child reinforced that belief. By this time, Paulette was involved in Christian prayer groups, and she decided to trust in the power of prayer. Despite her faith, she readily admits, "It was the longest nine months of my life."

To make matters worse, during her pregnancy the lupus spread to her heart and lungs, causing a flare-up that felt like a heart attack. She was rushed to the hospital, where they treated the inflammation with high doses of aspirin, which is now known to cause birth defects. Amazingly— perhaps miraculously—Paulette gave birth to a healthy baby daughter named Jackie in September 1977. Today, Jackie has been diagnosed with Attention Deficit Disorder, but she is in every other way a perfectly normal young woman.

In the spring of 1979, when Jackie was almost two years old, Paulette woke up in the middle of the night and told her husband that God wanted her to visit the cathedral of a television evangelist and faith healer named Ernest Angley in Akron, Ohio. He looked at her as though she was crazy and went back to sleep. They were struggling to pay for rent and food, let alone a trip to Ohio. But then, the very next day, they received a one hundred dollar check in the mail from an insurance company. It was just enough to pay for the trip.

Leaving the children with her parents, Paulette and her husband made the all-day drive to Akron. It was a hot day, and she got more sun through the car windows than was good for her. They had to save their money for gas and lodging, so they didn't eat much along the way, either. By the time they arrived at Angley's Grace Cathedral for the evening service, Paulette felt weak and nauseated, with excruciating pain in her joints.

"We proceeded to listen to this man beg for money for the next two hours," she remembers. "It was awful. It got to be nine o'clock and I was getting sicker and sicker." Paulette told her husband that she had to leave. She was heartbroken, for she felt she had come a long way for nothing. But she just couldn't make it through the service. Then something extraordinary happened—the beginning of a miracle.

"Just as I was getting ready to leave, he started calling people up for healing, and I was the third person that he called up. He pointed to me and said, 'Come down here and receive your miracle.' I just sat there. I couldn't even function, I couldn't even move. And he said, 'Don't you want to receive your healing?' And I just sat there, and all of a sudden I was on my feet, like somebody had lifted me. I didn't do it on my own. I know I didn't. So I got down there and was 'slain in the spirit' as they call it."

When Ernest Angley laid his hands upon Paulette for the healing, he said that she had an "arthritic-like condition," even though the only visible sign of her illness was the skin rash on her face. Despite this startling perception on the part of the faith healer, Paulette didn't feel any better. In fact, she woke up very early the next morning with the worst headache she could ever remember. Hoping to relieve the throbbing in her head, she settled into a warm bath and fell asleep in the tub. When her husband woke her two hours later, the water was cold and she felt strangely different. Then she realized that the pain in her joints was gone!

Since that morning, Paulette DeMauro has been completely free of the joint pains associated with lupus. At the same time, she also regained her old level of energy, allowing her to begin to lead a normal active life. At first, Paulette was convinced that she had been healed by Ernest Angley, and she became a committed follower of the evangelist. But then something happened that reminded her of the true source of her healing.

Although she no longer suffered from the joint pain and lethargy, Paulette still had the red skin rash on her face—the rash that had been the very first symptom that Halloween night. A year after the experience in Akron, Ernest Angley came to the Rochester area, and Paulette took her father to see him, hoping that the evangelist might heal him of his eye problems. But instead, Angley pointed to the section where they were sitting and said, "Somebody in this section has skin cancer. You've been told this is something else, but it's really skin cancer."

Convinced that he was talking about her, Paulette jumped to her feet and walked up toward the stage. But many others were there as well, and she politely let them go before her. The service ended with Paulette still standing in the line waiting to get up on the stage. She never came face-to-face with Angley to be "slain in the spirit" by the laying on of hands. Yet, within a week her rash disappeared as well—and it never came back. To Paulette this was a clear sign, a reminder that it is God who does the healing, not the faith healers and evangelists.

Today, twenty years after she was given six months to live, Paulette DeMauro is alive and well. She has worked in a variety of health care positions, first as an Emergency Medical Technician, then as a Registered Nurse. Her life has not been easy; she's weathered two divorces and recovered from a total hip replacement, due to bone degeneration caused by steroids used to control her lupus in the early years. Paulette hasn't taken medication for lupus for fifteen years, and she has no symptoms whatsoever. The official medical explanation for her remarkable recovery is "spontaneous remission," but Paulette says that she knows what really happened. She knows that she was healed by God.

Paulette has always wanted to share this healing power with others, both in her work as a medical professional and on a deeper, spiritual level. In 1992, she was ordained as a minister in a nondenominational Christian church dedicated to healing. Although she has no doubt that God can work through her if He wants to, she's not about to become another Ernest Angley. "I'm not real comfortable just walking up to people and saying, 'Hello, can I lay hands on you?'" she admits. "But I've found that when I pray for these people, and send healing white light to them, it seems to be working."

Paulette DeMauro's miraculous recovery from lupus is an impressive example of God's power. But to Paulette, it's only a small part of a greater, ongoing process of spiritual growth. "The biggest miracle of all," she says, "is just watching in hindsight the different things that have happened . . . and how they've brought me to the point that I'm at in my life and made me a more loving, accepting person."

TEARS, BLOOD, AND FATHER JIM

ON THANKSGIVING DAY 1991, FATHER JAMES BRUSE was visiting his parents at their home in Stafford, Virginia. Suddenly, the priest's mother, Ann Bruse, noticed drops of water forming on the face of a small plaster statue of Mary as Our Lady of Grace. "Jimmy, come here," she called to her son. "It's crying."

So began the strange, intriguing story of "Father Jim," a raw-boned priest with a thick black moustache, upswept hair, and a fondness for leather boots. Then in his late thirties, Bruse looked more like an aging football linebacker than a candidate for sainthood. Before that Thanksgiving, the most amazing accomplishment in his life was that he had once rode a roller coaster for five days straight, earning a mention in the *Guinness Book of Records*.

As a priest, Bruse was anything but a record-breaker. The assistant pastor of St. Elizabeth Ann Seton parish in the upscale suburb of Lake Ridge, Virginia, he flabbergasted the congregation with his rushed and stumbling sermons. Yet in the privacy of the confessional, he could be surprisingly warm and caring; he understood human imperfections because he was far from perfect himself. In fact, just a few days before the Thanksgiving visit, Father Jim had been lost in doubts about his vocation. The world of the spirit seemed so vague and ambiguous—he longed for a sign of God's presence in the world. "I don't know where to turn," he had prayed. "Please help me."

207

Then the statue began to cry. "There must be some explanation," said the priest's father. But though he turned the statue upside down and shook it, though he removed the jeweled halo and peered inside the statue's head with a flashlight and a magnifying glass, the tears continued to flow.

In the following days, four other statues in the Bruse home began to cry, emitting so much water that Mrs. Bruse had to place containers under them to protect the furniture. Sometimes the statues cried when the elder Bruses were alone or when no one was home, but the tears always appeared whenever their son Jim came to visit.

At first the Bruse family kept the strange occurrences to themselves. Then, on the day after Christmas, Father Jim felt sharp, stabbing pains in his wrists, and though the skin remained unbroken, blood began to flow. Later blood also appeared on his feet and his side. Although Jim didn't know what to think of the symptoms, his mother recognized the signs of stigmata. She suggested that he discuss the situation with "Father Dan," Father Daniel Hamilton, pastor of Seton parish.

On New Year's Eve, Father Jim went to Father Dan's office in the rectory and poured out his tale of weeping statues and strange bleeding. The elder priest was understandably skeptical, but he decided to trade statues with his assistant as a sort of experiment. He also offered to find a copy of the *Catholic Encyclopedia* so that Father Jim could read more about stigmata.

A few hours later, when he stopped by the younger priest's bedroom to drop off the encyclopedia, Father Dan stared in amazement at the statue of St. Elizabeth Ann Seton, the statue he had loaned his assistant earlier. Although Father Jim was not in the room, the statue was crying tears that looked like blood. When Father Dan returned to his own room, he discovered that the statue of Mary that Father Jim had loaned him was also crying—and the crying continued all the next day through the long parade of New Year's bowl games that the priest watched on TV.

Father Dan reported the situation to Bishop John R. Keating of the Arlington Diocese, who told him to keep the story quiet and have Jim examined by a physician. A few days later, when Father Jim and Father Dan visited Bishop Keating, a statue of Mary on the bishop's mantle began to cry. Still Keating was hesitant to publicize the story, even after an internist and a psychiatrist both reported that they could find nothing medically or psychologically wrong with the young priest.

All efforts at secrecy ended on March 1, 1992, when the big Madonna in St. Elizabeth Ann Seton church began to weep in front of five hundred parishioners during Father Jim's celebration of the Mass. Local news and television reporters jumped on the story, and the following Sunday, 3,000 people tried to crowd into the church, causing such a traffic jam that county police officers had to be called to the scene.

In the weeks that followed, statues seemed to weep wherever Father Jim went and rumors of miracles blew through the quiet Virginia suburb like a spiritual whirlwind. Some people said they saw spinning suns and rays of colored light, or rosaries that changed hues before their eyes. Others claimed to be healed miraculously by Father Jim's touch. An eight-year-old girl with curvature of the spine exhibited extraordinary improvement after being blessed by the priest, her curvature reduced from eighteen degrees to four degrees. But it was hard to say whether the improvement was due to Father Jim Bruse or the plastic body cast that she wore twenty-three hours a day. For the girl herself, however, the answer was easy. "I really believe it was Father Bruse."

On orders from Bishop Keating, Father Bruse stopped talking with the press, and the miracle furor began to die down. The stigmatic bleeding stopped, as did the weeping of the big statue in the church. But a year later—when the story appeared in a national news magazine—smaller statues continued to weep in Father Jim's presence, and reports of healings continued as well. Father Jim Bruse no longer questioned his vocation and spent his extra time ministering to the sick.

"We don't have to worry about what's beyond death," he told a friend. "We know. It's total love."

A Man in Black

The mother in this story has passed away, but her two sons remember this remarkable event as clearly as if it were yesterday.

As the winter of 1955 swept into Detroit, Florence faced a bleak and frightening reality. Her husband, Jack, had been sent to prison earlier that year, leaving her to care for their twin seven-year-old boys, Tom and Gerry. Before he went away, Jack bought her a small restaurant as a way to support herself. But Florence didn't really know anything about the business, and the restaurant failed. Now she had run out of money. She couldn't pay her heating bills; she couldn't even put food on the table for her two sons.

A traditional '50s homemaker with little experience in the job market, Florence was at a loss. She didn't know what to do or where to turn. For a long time, she just sat at the kitchen table and cried, with her young sons watching in fear and wonder. Then, through her tears, she began to pray.

Florence was a deeply spiritual person, but she didn't go to church on Sunday or follow a conventional religious belief. Her relationship with God was more personal, almost like a friendship. She believed that God was with her all the time, listening and watching out for her and her family. So now, in her fear and sorrow, she poured out her heart to God, her friend, almost as if He were sitting there beside her at the kitchen table.

Suddenly there was a knock on the door. Quickly wiping her tears, Florence went to open it and discovered an old man dressed in black, but without a clergyman's collar or any other identifying sign. She had never seen him before. Without saying a word, the man simply handed her an envelope and walked away.

When Florence opened the envelope, she discovered five hundred dollars! In those days, it was a small fortune, more than enough to get them through the winter.

Florence never saw the man in black again, and never found out who he was. But he came to her at the very moment she needed him most, at the moment she prayed to God—her friend.

THE TOUCH
OF THE MUSE

Ann's mother pulled the covers up and kissed her lightly on the cheek. Then she turned away and disappeared without a word, leaving Ann all alone in the dark. It was November 1953, and Ann was just four years old.

Frightened, she pulled the covers up over her head, hoping to hide from whatever strange horrors lurked in the darkness. Suddenly the room was lit by a strange glow—bright enough that she could see it through the covers. Cautiously, curiously, the little girl pulled the covers down and stared in terror at a woman sitting in a chair at the foot of the bed. Or at least it looked like a woman. She was wearing a skirt and a blouse, and she had reddish-brown shoulder length hair. But her face was not normal. It was vague and gaseous, like a glowing sphere.

The woman did not speak, but Ann "knew" that she was going to stand up and walk over to the bed. And so she did, sitting down beside her. Now Ann could make out her features: fine, light, luminous skin with piercing blue eyes and a full, oval face. She seemed to be in her early thirties, about the age of Ann's own mother.

Still the woman said nothing. But she smiled gently at the frightened girl, a half-smile really, a "Mona Lisa" smile. And once again, without words, Ann knew what the woman would do next. She would reach out and touch her on the arm, and Ann would feel electricity.

As soon as this thought registered in Ann's mind, the woman did exactly as she expected, reaching out and gently touching her on the arm. But the jolt of electricity was not gentle at all; it was powerful, painful, and frightening. It only lasted a moment. Then without a word, the woman stood up from the bed and walked out through a wall in Ann's room.

At first, Ann told no one about this experience. Overwhelming for a four-year-old, she repressed it in the layers of her mind. But a few years later, after her family had moved to a new house, the experience came back to her. It began with a strange mental sensation, what Ann now calls a "textural memory," as if someone were drawing heavy lines across a piece of paper. As Ann tried to understand this strange sensation, the encounter with the woman became clearer until she could remember it as distinctly as if it had happened only a moment before. But now—perhaps because she was a few years older, perhaps because she lived in a different place—she was able to accept the experience and let it become a part of her life.

Today, over forty years after the encounter in her darkened room, Ann is a professional pianist who has performed as a soloist with major orchestras and graced the stages of New York concert halls. She believes that the touch of the glowing woman changed her life, opening a new channel of searching and spirituality within her—a guiding hand in the development of her musical career.

"I'd hate to sound as if I've won the 'spiritual awareness award' with my musical interpretations," Ann says today, "but I'm more directed to searching and conveying the higher spiritual plane of a composition than most. . . . I believe the gift from the angel was a spiritual source that has directed me to music as the medium for my life."

For centuries, poets, musicians, and artists have described inspiration as the "touch of the muse." Most of us have always assumed that this touch was metaphorical, an image to represent a kind of inspiration that we cannot explain in words. But for Ann, this touch was more than a metaphor, it was a palpable, even painful, jolt of electricity from a glowing woman who appeared at the foot of her bed.

A VISIBLE SIGN

Sometimes the greatest significance of a miracle is simply to remind us that God is listening. Take this heartwarming story of a family in Chattanooga, Tennessee.

FOR AS LONG AS THEY COULD REMEMBER, REGIS AND Joanne Nicoll had been trying to find a way to explain their faith in God to their daughter, Devon. Although only eleven years old, she was a bright young lady who asked probing, difficult questions—questions that have challenged philosophers for thousands of years. How can we be sure God exists? If God does exit, why doesn't He make it clear to us? How do we know that God answers or even hears our prayers? If He does seem to answer our prayers, how do we know it's not just a coincidence?

Concerned about their daughter's spiritual growth, Regis and Joanne made an interesting and unusual decision. They decided to pray for a reason to pray—asking God to give them something very specific that they could pray for as a family, so that Devon could see that God really did answer her prayers. As Regis later explained, "Little did I suspect how He would do this."

In November 1994, the Nicoll family was returning home from the weekly Saturday service at their Seventh Day Adventist church. It was a clear sunny day with the temperature in the mid-forties, typical late-fall weather in Chattanooga, Tennessee. As Regis guided the car up their steep driveway, they felt two distinct "bumps," almost as if the car had run over a pile of large tree branches. But the piercing canine cry that followed made it clear what had really happened.

"Oh, my God!" Regis exclaimed as he turned off the ignition, "I've run over Simon!" Simon was their big, beloved, ten-year-old black mutt. Instantly, the family was thrown into a state of panic, with Devon and her younger brother Alex in tears, and Regis and Joanne screaming and shifting into a crisis mode. Joanne got out of the car first, and her screams intensified when she discovered Simon still pinned beneath one of the rear wheels.

"Everyone out of the car now!" Regis shouted. "Now! Out! Out! Out!" As the children scrambled out of the back seat, he tried to restart the car and put it in reverse in order to free Simon from beneath the wheel. But in the panic of the moment, he couldn't get the key to turn. "My only thought," he remembers, "was to get Simon to the vet quickly, so he could be put to sleep before he suffered too much."

Finally the car started, and Regis backed up just enough to free Simon from the wheel. He got out and ran over to the side where Simon lay, but the dog was motionless. Regis assumed he was paralyzed with a broken back. Again, his only thought was to get the dog to the veterinarian to have him put out of his misery.

In the meantime, Joanne had taken the two children into the house where they began praying that Simon would live and be all right. As Regis admits, "This certainly would *not* have been the prayer I would have encouraged, had I been the one in the house with the kids . . . the outcome of this situation seemed all too clear to me at the time." Nonetheless, while their father was outside with his doubts, the children and their mother continued to pray. Joanne later told Regis that Devon's prayer was especially loud and passionate.

Regis reached under the car and tried to pull Simon from underneath the chassis, still assuming he was paralyzed. But to the man's amazement, the big black dog began to wiggle and squirm, until he finally freed himself from the car. He stood up and walked down the driveway, without a limp and with no apparent injury. Awestruck, Regis followed the dog into the front yard. Just then the mail truck pulled up to their mailbox, and Simon ran down toward the street, barking at the mailman, just as if nothing had ever happened.

"The whole family—and especially Devon—knows that God worked a miracle in our lives that day," Regis explains. "Since then, Devon has affirmed several times to us and some friends how God answered her prayer."

For a doubting eleven-year-old girl, the fact that God answered her prayer to save her dog must be a powerful, faith-building experience. And perhaps that experience will make a positive difference in the life of Devon Nicoll. But in many ways, the real miracle occurred for her father, Regis. After all, he had been struggling to explain the concept of faith to Devon, yet he had nothing but doubts as he looked at Simon pinned beneath the car. At that moment, he was convinced that the outcome of the accident was "all too clear," convinced that there was nothing he could do except take Simon to the vet and have him put to sleep. But the outcome wasn't clear at all—not as far as God was concerned.

"The whole episode has awakened me to the truth that God wants nothing more than to see our faith grow in Him," Regis says today. "And He'll go to some extravagant measures to convince us of His love and character. His message to me is that no request is too bold, or the outcome of a prayer too obvious, to expect God to reveal Himself."

DECEMBER

It came upon the midnight clear,
That glorious song of old,
From angels bending near the earth
To touch their harps of gold . . .

—EDMUND HAMILTON SEARS,
"THE ANGEL'S SONG"

CHRISTMAS MUSIC

The great Welsh poet, Dylan Thomas, wrote a famous story called "A Child's Christmas in Wales." Perhaps you have read this story—or even better—heard a recording of Thomas reading it in his deep, rolling voice. The first time I heard the story, I was instantly caught in its wonder and magic. This is the story of another child and another Christmas in Wales, and though not as long or as lyrical as Thomas's tale, it's just as magical.

In the village of Talyllyn lived the family of Tudor Llewellyn Henry John. Now Talyllyn is located about five miles from Brecon, which is the heart of the Brecon Beacons—a cluster of rolling green mountains that are covered by sheep most of the year, with an added dose of wild daffodils in the spring and fresh snow in the winter. The John family lived in an old two-story stone house with ivy crawling up one side and twenty-four apple trees in the back garden.

The John family was living proof of a very special love—the love between enemies in war. Mr. John had been captured by the Germans during World War II and had met his German-born wife, Brunhilde, while a prisoner-of-war. They survived the bombing of Dresden together, and Brunhilde helped her beloved Welshman to escape. When the war was over, despite the objections of her own mother, the young German woman returned to Wales with him, where they married and settled down in Talyllyn. In time they had four daughters: Cristel, Monica, Karin, and Caroline. Karin later emigrated to the United States, and it is she who tells this story.

It was Christmas Eve 1959, and the John family sat around the tree in their cozy front room, opening their presents. As Karin remembers, "It was simple and simply wonderful . . . in those days we were happy with new mittens, a little doll, a box of chocolates." Suddenly they heard the strains of a beautiful Christmas carol playing on a piano in their kitchen. Yet, as far as they knew, they were all alone in the house!

The whole family went to investigate, leaving the warmth of their cozy tree and walking down the hallway, past the stairs, through the dining room and up to the closed door that led into the kitchen. For a moment, they all paused outside the door, listening to the beautiful music filled with the simple joy of Christmas. They all heard it— the four girls and their parents as well. Who could it be, playing their piano?

Karin was seven years old at the time; today, over thirty-five years later she recalls the magic of the moment: "As we stood at the door, listening to the piano, I remember feeling a sense of total awe, convinced that when I opened the door, I was going to see an angel."

Slowly and carefully, Mr. John opened the door and the whole family stared in wonder at the sight. There was no angel—at least not an angel they could see. There was no one at all. Only a piano, playing beautiful Christmas music all by itself.

For Karin John, this was the beginning of a lifetime of contact with a reality beyond the physical world. A few years later, when she went away to boarding school at the age of ten, she *did* see an angel. Coming from such a close, loving family, she was naturally traumatized at being separated from her parents. One night, she saw an angel standing at the foot of her bed.

"She stood there quietly and non-threatening," Karin remembers, "and I stared at her, waiting for her to disappear as things you see at night usually do—when you look long enough. She wouldn't go away, and then I became scared and dove under the blanket. I waited about a minute and looked again. She was still there. I went back under the blanket and waited about five minutes, and when I came up again, she was gone."

As an adult Karin has had many incidents of extraordinary premonitions and dreams. But of all her experiences, the piano that played by itself made the strongest impression on her. For though she encountered other people who had premonitions, and even some who had seen angels, she never came across another story of a piano playing by itself.

Then, about a year ago, she happened to buy a book near her home in Michigan, and she was amazed to discover a story about a piano playing all alone. In this case, the piano was in a house where the man next door had recently died—and the dead man had been a piano player. But the most amazing aspect of all is that the house was located in the town of Merthyr Tydfil, which is just across the beacons from Karin's home village of Talyllyn.

Do pianos play by themselves? In Wales they do.

AN ANGEL
ON MY SHOULDER

*I lost three friends to AIDS in 1994, all beautiful, creative
people who passed before their time. So though I never
knew Jim, this story has special meaning for me.*

SUE FIRST NOTICED JIM AT A GRADE SCHOOL ASSEMBLY
in her small Wyoming hometown. Chosen to play a piano
solo, he performed the "Theme from Exodus" with great
crashing chords and a theatrical flourish that impressed the
whole school—though Sue remembers that many students
thought playing the piano was pretty silly for a boy. This
was the early 1960s, and people in small-town America still
had definite ideas about what boys and girls should do.

As they progressed through junior high and high school,
Sue's path occasionally crossed with Jim's through their
mutual interest in band, choir, and drama. They both played
piano and were often called upon to serve as accompanists.
But Sue was three years older, so they were never really
close—acquaintances and occasional colleagues, but not
friends.

Sue went away to college and spent two years with a
traveling theater company. Then, in 1976, she moved to
New York City, light years from small-town Wyoming. She
vaguely remembered some mutual friends mentioning that
Jim lived somewhere in Greenwich Village, so she looked

him up in the phone book, and sure enough there was a listing. It turned out that Jim lived right around the corner from her, and he came over in the blink of an eye.

From that day on, Sue and Jim were fast friends. The age difference didn't matter anymore. They were both young adults, far from their families, embarking on an exciting, challenging voyage of exploration and self-discovery. For Jim, these were the difficult, yet intriguing years of "coming out" as a gay man, and Sue was there to offer her unconditional support. But the way Sue sees it today, Jim more than paid her back with his own friendship and insightful, delightful view of the world.

"Jim took care of me, always, as he did all his other friends. He was always there for me. We had wonderful times together. His humor and sense of play about life were infectious and always healed one's troubles. He remembered every detail of your life, even the ones you forgot, and would sometimes ask about a thing years later—or remind you of something silly you had done!"

Sue left New York for a couple of years, and by the time she returned, Jim had found a devoted lover and settled into a country house. At first she spent time there, but gradually they saw less of each other, not because of any breach in their friendship, but simply because they were busy people building their lives. With his restless, creative intelligence, Jim tried a variety of careers, always earning enough to supply his modest needs. His real career, Sue believes, was his friends. And she was one of them. As the years passed, they kept in touch, and though months might go by between conversations, she always felt as if she had just talked with him yesterday.

By the early 1990s, Jim had developed AIDS and his life became one potentially fatal illness after another. Sue didn't spend much time physically with him during his illnesses, because she felt that she would only be another burden. She knew that Jim would want to take care of his friends no matter how sick he was himself. So instead of visiting in person, they had long, wonderful telephone conversations.

In her own career as a hospital nutrition counselor, Sue worked with many terminally ill patients, and she had plenty of experience with death and dying. So she would ask Jim how he *really* felt, not only physically, but mentally and spiritually. And she was always impressed with the clear-thinking courage with which he approached his illness. The body can create natural painkillers, he told her, that are more powerful than any drug. And as for the time beyond the pain, he said simply and honestly that he wasn't afraid of death.

AIDS does not kill quickly. It's a long, slow agonizing process of illness followed by recovery followed by illness, with the very real possibility that each illness will be the last. Through it all, Jim maintained his playful personality, more easily than those who loved him. Once when he lay critically ill and unconscious in his hospital bed, with his friends and family gathered tearfully around him, he regained consciousness for a moment and told everyone to lighten up and turn on MTV! Later, when he recovered from this particular brush with death, he felt bad for hurting everyone's feelings. He knew they meant well. But the way Jim saw it, MTV was better than tears.

Jim died in December 1992. At the memorial service, a long parade of friends and family testified to the impact that he had made on their lives. The testimony went on for two hours. Although Sue was well aware of Jim's capacity for caring and friendship, she found herself overwhelmed by the magnitude and intensity of that friendship. "The testimony at his memorial service as to how he had changed so many lives—basically just by being there and being always a beacon of love—was the most amazing thing I've ever witnessed."

Sue admits that she was devastated by Jim's death, despite her professional experience. Not that he was really a daily part of her life; that aspect of their friendship had passed long ago. Her own sense of loss was deeper and more abstract. "I was devastated because he was such a pure soul and he suffered, and I would miss just always knowing he was there for me if I needed him."

Then, two days after the memorial service, something amazing happened to help her with her grief. Sue was walking down a street in her New York City neighborhood, going to her lawyer's office, when Jim's voice "popped" out of nowhere and began to speak to her, as clearly as if he were alive. She couldn't see him, but the voice was undeniable, "like an angel on my shoulder."

"Lighten up!" he said. "I'm OK! It's really fun here. . . . Enjoy the moment. . . . You'll have fun when you get here, too. . . . Don't worry about it. . . . You're gonna love it. . . . You'll understand when you get here."

Jim's voice continued to speak to her for about ten days, whenever she found herself overwhelmed by sadness over his death. And today, over two years later, Sue can still call up his voice when she needs it. The message is always the same: Enjoy each moment in this life and don't worry about death, because you'll enjoy the afterlife, too.

It seems as if Jim—the man who always took care of his friends—is taking care of Sue even after his death. "This experience was so real for me," she writes, "that it healed my pain over his death very quickly. He restores my sense of humor with his own inimitable humor. And the gift that he gave me was a much stronger belief in the afterlife. . . . It's shocking to me, but it's true."

RIDERS IN THE
SNOW

The following story was passed on to me by Conger Beasley, who participated in the 100th anniversary Big Foot Memorial Ride. Conger heard the story directly from Alex White Plume.

IN DECEMBER 1890, THE GREAT LAKOTA CHIEF SITTING Bull was killed by Indian policemen sent by a U.S. government agent to arrest him. Refugees from Sitting Bull's camp then joined the followers of another Lakota chief named Big Foot. Fearing that he and his people might be arrested as well, Big Foot led them on a one hundred-mile flight across the rugged Badlands of South Dakota, until they were stopped by soldiers of the Seventh Cavalry, the division once commanded by Custer at the Little Big Horn.

The soldiers ordered Big Foot's band to follow them to a camp along Wounded Knee Creek, where they surrounded the Indians and trained four Hotchkiss machine guns on the camp. On the morning of December 29—exactly two weeks after the death of Sitting Bull—the Seventh Cavalry demanded that Big Foot's people give up their guns.

There are many versions of what happened next, but this much is certain: The soldiers of the Seventh Cavalry opened fire on Big Foot's band with the machine guns, and the camp became a bloodbath. When it was over, 146 Indians lay dead along the creek, including forty-four women and eighteen children. Perhaps thirty or forty others staggered away to die elsewhere. Twenty-five soldiers were also killed.

The government called the conflict the Battle of Wounded Knee, and tried to portray it as the last great battle between the American Indians and the U.S. Army. But in the eyes of the Indian people, and especially in the eyes of the Lakota, it was not a battle at all. It was a massacre—symptomatic and symbolic of the federal government's systematic efforts to destroy their culture and steal their land.

Almost a century later, the Lakota decided to retrace the journey of Big Foot and his followers across the Badlands to the fateful encampment at Wounded Knee. For the twentieth century Lakota, it was a way of honoring their ancestors and coming to terms with their own grief and anger over the wrongs of the past. The first Big Foot Memorial Ride was held in 1986, with the fifth and final ride held in 1990, the 100th anniversary of Wounded Knee.

It was on the second ride, however, in December 1987, that something miraculous occurred. There were thirty-six riders that year, and the weather was cold and snowy. After three days, the ride had fallen behind schedule, so they decided to continue into the night to make up for lost time.

An hour or so after darkness had settled over the Badlands, Alex White Plume, one of the leaders of the ride, noticed strange, glowing sparks around the horses' hooves. He and another leader, Rocky Afraid of Hawk, decided to go to the head of the line and count the riders as they passed, to make sure that no one had fallen too far behind or gotten lost on the dark, snowy trail. By this time, the sparks from the horses' hooves were as dense as fireflies.

As the two men counted the riders, the line seemed to go on and on. The silhouettes of many riders appeared strangely jagged and misshapen, as if they were wearing buffalo robes or furs and carrying staffs or lances. But strangest of all was the count. Both Alex and Rocky counted eighty-six riders—fifty more than they expected, fifty more than they had last counted in the daylight. By the time the last rider passed, the hair on the back of Alex White Plume's neck stood straight with awe. He was watching the passage of his ancestors.

An hour later, when the line of riders reached their camp for the night, Alex and Rocky counted them again. This time there were only thirty-six. The others—the old ones—had faded into the night.

2000 ANGELS

*Andy Lakey's story has been featured on a long parade
of television shows, from Oprah Winfrey to CNN and
NBC. The story below is based on personal interviews,
and represents the most complete version of his experiences to date. Amazingly—perhaps miraculously—Andy
is married to Chantal, whose own story is told in "Angels
in the Mist," in January; yet they met years after their
angel encounters.*

ANDY LAKEY WAS ON THE FAST TRACK TO NOWHERE.
At the age of twenty-seven, he was already a successful
salesman, making more money than people twice his age.
But he spent it as fast as it came in—and most of it he
spent on drugs. Andy had started smoking marijuana in
junior high and his drug use escalated over the years. Now
he was heavily into cocaine, snorting and free-basing. It
was the free-basing that really got him. When he smoked
the potent solution, it seemed to take over his entire being.
He lived to base; he based to live. And it was killing him.

On New Year's Eve 1986, Andy went to a party at a
friend's apartment just upstairs from his own. Naturally
there was coke, and Andy snorted a few lines and smoked
some base. Even though it was New Year's Eve, he didn't
really do any more drugs than usual. In fact, there were
plenty of times when he had done more. But on this particular evening, the drugs affected him differently. ''I felt

very strange," he later remembered, "like my body was about to shut down. I felt like I was dying."

The smart thing would have been to tell his friends to call 911. But Andy was too macho for that; he didn't want to die in front of everyone. So he struggled to his feet and pulled himself together enough to say good-bye. Then he stumbled out the door and fell down the stairs, picked himself up again and stumbled into his own apartment. He decided to make a can of Campbell's tomato soup and managed to pour the can into a pot on the stove. But he doesn't remember whether he ever turned on the flame. What he does remember is this: he felt a powerful and sudden instinct to get into the shower. And so he did, not even bothering to take off his clothes.

As he stood under the cold running water, Andy began to pray—the first time he had prayed since he was a little boy. "Please, God, I'm sorry for my sins, and I want to go to heaven." It was a natural prayer for a man who thought he was dying. But as the cold water cascaded over his body, he prayed for something else. He prayed for life. "If you let me live, I'll never do drugs again. And I'll do something to help children, to help mankind."

Instantly Andy Lakey felt a presence, "a swirling sensation around my feet, like a rapid tornado getting faster and faster. There were seven figures around me that I had never seen before. I thought maybe I *was* going to heaven. These seven figures kept twirling around me, rising to my chest area. Then they all came into one, and put their arms around me."

Now Andy found himself in another dimension, far from the earthly reality of his shower. He saw a huge ball of light—like a brilliant sun—with giant poles of light extending outward from its center. The outer shell of the poles was translucent gold set against the infinite blackness of the void. And through the translucence he could see countless forms traveling toward the ball of light as if they were climbing a heavenly escalator.

He knew instinctively that these forms were the souls of

those who were passing from one plane of existence to the next, but there were so many of them—billions upon billions it seemed—that they couldn't possibly be only the souls of those who were dying on the earth. They must be all the souls of the universe, perhaps the souls of every sentient being. He didn't know. But whatever they were, he wanted to join them. He wanted to enter one of the translucent poles and rise upward toward the heavens. But he couldn't get in. He tried and tried again, only to bounce off the outer surface.

"I was bounced out or rejected," he explains today. "There was a definite refusal to grant me entrance. I kept trying and trying, and that's when I woke up in the hospital."

The first sensations that brought Andy back to the earthly world were the raw pain in his throat from having his stomach pumped and the sharp IV needles in his arms. Gradually he learned what had happened "on the outside." After stumbling into his apartment, he had left the door opened. A friend from the party decided to check on him and found Andy's body frozen and rigid on the floor of the shower, with the cold water still cascading over him. The friend called another friend, and together they managed to get Andy into a car and rush him to the hospital, fortunately only a few blocks away.

Andy Lakey's near-death experience is vivid, intriguing, and powerful. But it's not that different from hundreds of near-death experiences that have been reported and recorded over the years. And by itself, perhaps, a near-death experience is not necessarily a miracle. The real miracle is how this experience changed Andy's life, and ultimately how it changed the lives of others.

Andy Lakey kept his vow to never do drugs again. When he recovered, he returned to his sales job with a new obsession, working double shifts to make up for the money he had wasted in the past. When he wasn't working, he began to draw. Although he had no formal artistic training, he had always been a compulsive doodler, but now his "doodling" took on new meaning. It was an effort to heal himself and understand his experience. Again and again he tried to draw the forms of the seven angels that had swirled around him in the shower. They were not at all like the angels he had seen in books and paintings. No wings, no faces—just pure, powerful forms. During the next four years, Andy made 236 drawings of these forms, trying to capture and communicate what he had seen.

Then in October 1989, on his thirtieth birthday, Andy Lakey made a startling choice. He decided to quit his sales job and become a painter. He had never painted before, and he knew nothing about the world of professional art. But he knew that he had to paint. And he sensed that somehow his painting would be a way to keep his second promise to God—the promise to do something to help other people, especially children.

That year Andy made $85,000 as a salesman. When he told his boss that he wanted to quit and become an artist, the other man naturally concluded that he was crazy. He suggested that Andy see a corporate psychologist, but Andy was adamant. He was following a different kind of guidance. So he quit his job, bought some painting supplies, and began to turn the garage of his newly-purchased condominium into a studio.

By New Year's Eve 1989, the studio was ready and Andy sat down to paint. "But it didn't work," he recalls simply. Of course only a person with enormous faith—or enormous naiveté—would expect it to work. After all, he was a complete novice trying to capture pure form and heavenly light, a subject that had teased the masters for centuries.

A few days later—Andy thinks it was January 3, 1990—he went down to his studio and turned the light on. He had it hooked up so that the radio came on with the light, and the first song he heard was the Rolling Stones' "Satisfaction," he remembers today, fully aware of the irony. Suddenly he felt an unseen hand push him back against the wall, and he began to meditate, though he'd never meditated before and has never meditated since. He gazed downward for a moment, and when he lifted his eyes he saw a ball of light coming at him through the wall.

"The ball of light . . . hit me in the forehead and surrounded my body," Andy remembers. He saw three angels, but they weren't like the angels in his near-death experience. They were men in beards—like the three angels described in the biblical story of Abraham. "They told me they wanted me to become an artist and paint two thousand angels by the year two thousand. They didn't tell me why, but they said they'd give me the knowledge to paint and they would make circumstances available for me to be successful—because they had plans for me, for this art. Then they went away and said they'd visit me again in the year two thousand."

Actually, Andy admits, the three angels didn't "say" these things, and he's not sure if they spoke at all. But they communicated the message clearly. For Andy, the experience seemed to last a lifetime. But when the angels disappeared, "Satisfaction" was still playing on the radio.

"I knew what to do," Andy remembers. "I took most of the supplies back to the art store, because I didn't need them. And the next day I started my first painting."

That first painting now hangs beside the front door of Andy's home. It portrays the seven angels Andy saw in the shower as pure forms filled with strong, raised, maze-like lines, establishing a unique style that Andy has continued to develop. I am not an art critic, and most art critics find it difficult to categorize or describe Andy's art. But I would call his style cosmic primitive relief.

Andy Lakey finished five paintings in the month of January. Instinctively, he felt that he should go hang one of his paintings at the bank across the street from his studio. The painting he chose did not include any of the angel forms, but it was in the same style as the angel paintings. The bank manager, Linda, gave him permission to hang it, and that day an art collector from Canada happened to come into the bank on business. Linda later told Andy that the Canadian visitor stood and stared at his painting for almost an hour.

In an effort to find out more about the artist, the collector contacted a local art consultant named Pierrette Van Cleve who came to visit Andy in his studio. She too was impressed by his work, and at first she refused to believe that he had only been painting for three weeks. Noting the raised texture of his forms, Van Cleve suggested that Andy share his work with the blind. Andy realized that this was a way to begin keeping his second promise—the promise to help mankind. So a show was quickly arranged, with the blind visitors encouraged to touch the paintings, feeling the art that they couldn't see with their eyes.

The story of a painter who could speak to the blind was told by television and other media throughout the country. The day of Andy's first show, network anchorman Peter Jennings happened to be in San Diego, and Andy gave him one of his paintings, which Jennings took back to New York and donated to the Lighthouse for the Blind. By mid-February 1990, only six weeks after he began his first painting, Andy Lakey was on the road to success on both coasts.

Today Andy Lakey's paintings are sold by more than sixty galleries in the United States and Canada. Each gallery is required to donate a percentage of gross sales to a local charity dedicated to helping children, and Andy often donates his paintings to charitable causes. Among those who have acquired Andy's paintings—for their own collections and as donations to hospitals or homes for the blind—are ex-Presidents Ronald Reagan, Gerald Ford and Jimmy Carter; Prince Albert of Monaco; singers Ray Charles, Stevie Wonder, Gloria Estefan, and Naomi Judd; and actors Henry Winkler and Ed Asner. Andy's first "celebrity client" was Pope John Paul II, who gratefully accepted one of his angel paintings for the Vatican.

But Andy Lakey's art is more than a miraculous success story. It is also a story of healing and helping others. Andy has received over 60,000 letters from people who have been touched by his life and his work. Some have stopped doing drugs; some have been consoled after the loss of a loved one; some simply want to share their own experiences with angels. He has also received extraordinary reports from people who truly believe they were healed by his paintings. For Andy, that's what it's all about. "You may change the life of one person," he says, "who gives birth to someone who finds the cure for cancer. You never know. So I'm just going with the flow, painting my angel paintings, and we'll just see what the next step is."

Since the vision of the three bearded men, Andy has progressed well over halfway toward his goal of creating 2,000 angel paintings by the year 2000. On New Year's Eve 1999, he plans to have a party in New York City for those who have bought his paintings, and he will place the finishing touch on the final angel. What will happen then? Will the three angels return? And if so, what will they tell him? Andy Lakey just smiles and shrugs. "I'll have to wait till the year two thousand."

Have You Been Touched
by a Miracle?

If you or someone you know has experienced a miracle that you would like to share in a future book, please contact me at the following address:

Paul Robert Walker
P.O. Box 301171
Escondido, California 92030

Tell me when and where the miracle happened, and as many details as you can remember. Be sure to give me a way to contact you in order to discuss the story further—an address, phone number, fax number, and/or e-mail address. I will not publish a story without a follow-up contact.

I'll send an autographed copy of the book to anyone whose story I use in a future collection.

May your life always be touched by miracles!

PAUL ROBERT WALKER has written more than a dozen books on a wide variety of subjects, including biographies, histories, novels and folktales. His work has been honored by the National Council for the Social Studies, the Children's Book Council, the American Folklore Society and *American Bookseller*. A former high school teacher, journalist, and reference editor, Mr. Walker travels throughout the country, sharing his stories and writing experiences with other writers, teachers and students. He is a member of the Authors Guild, PEN Center West and the Society of Children's Book Writers and Illustrators. Mr. Walker lives in Escondido, California, with his wife and children.